FULL CONTACT KICKBOXING

A complete guide to training and strategies

Andy Dumas & James Turner

FULL CONTACT KICKBOXING

A complete guide to training and strategies

THE CROWOOD PRESS

First published in 2022 by
The Crowood Press Ltd
Ramsbury, Marlborough
Wiltshire SN8 2HR

enquiries@crowood.com
www.crowood.com

British Library Cataloguing-in-Publication Data
A catalogue record for this book is available from the British Library.

ISBN 978 0 7198 4139 2

Cover design: Sergey Tsvetkov

Photo credits
Instructional photographs by Kyla McCall, Nikola Novak, Troy Moth, Anna Tarazevich and Mark Yeomans. James Turner fight photographs by Katie Bater Photography, Stewart Lee – Instant Memories, and Mark Yeomans Photography. Photo consultant: Kyla McCall.

Dedication
Dedicated to our parents, Eve and Cliff Dumas Sr, and Kay and Andrew Turner.

Acknowledgements
Our thanks go to Scott Ashley, Paul Barnett (UK Martial Arts Show), John Barrett (JBAMA), Chad Blevins, Massimo Brizi (IKTA Italia/Vice World President), Curtis Bush, Alessio Crescentini, Brenda DiTullio, Steve and Jill Dowrick, Jamie Dumas, Louise Fletcher (Cornwall College Sport), Shingo Fukoshima, Marco Ghibaudo (IKTA World President), Richie Hale, Zoltan Horvath, Jackie Jenks, Jack Johns, Angie LaFontaine, Gemma Mitchell, Dorian Murray, Kyle 'Like Whoa' Murray, 'Iron' Ron Murray, Tracy Murray, Carl 'Nevercease' Noel, Laecio Nunes, Gyula T. Pap, Abi Perkins, Sophie Prideaux, Andrea Rinaldi, Dan Sillifant, Gary Sillifant, Dave Steggles, Bob Sykes (UK Martial Arts Show), Lee Toms, Mandy Tredinnick, George Turner, Aleksandr Usmanov, Bill 'Superfoot' Wallace, Bernie Willems, Don 'The Dragon' Wilson, James Wilson, Mark Yeomans. Andy Dumas/James Turner artwork by Jōnetsu. If we've left your name out, remind us, and we'll get you in the next book!

Evolve Sport and Fitness Camborne, Cornwall College Sport; S.W.A.T. Health (Synergy Wellness Attitude Training), Port Credit, Ontario; Lowell MacLean of www.apex-fitness.ca; www.rootsoffight.com.

Typeset by Simon and Sons
Printed and bound in India by Replika Press

Contents

Foreword
by World Champion Massimo Brizi

When one begins learning Kickboxing or any combat sport, it often happens on a whim or without much enthusiasm. But after several lessons, the student tends to change in attitude, being fascinated by the various techniques that are gradually introduced over the proceeding weeks and months. Continuing regular training, the student experiences the satisfaction that comes through physical improvement acquired in a short time. When this change in attitude occurs, the student decides to persevere with awareness of what can be achieved. The student chooses to embark on a path....

Massimo Brizi and Alessio Panetta.

Over time, this awareness becomes deeper, as we begin to look beyond the technical skills and physical training, and we perceive that these two aspects of Martial Arts are intimately related to the mind. Therefore, our mental attitude comes into play and is cultivated through training for improvements in physical performance and technical skill. Combat sport is therefore transformed for many into the ideal habitat where technique, physical training and mental exercise become tools for inner growth. Those who truly follow the path of combat look after the roots of the plant more than its flowers.

Within the pages of this book, you will learn, step-by-step, the process for attaining proficiency in the art and sport of Kickboxing. All the elements of offence, defence, tactics, physical training and mental approach are covered by co-authors who are acclaimed experts in the combat sports world.

Andy Dumas is a prolific individual in the field, having authored several successful Boxing training books and videos throughout a career spanning over 20 years. He is highly respected in fight sports and the fitness industry. From a young age, Andy learned Boxing from his father, Cliff Dumas Sr. who was Canadian Champion. Andy's lifelong passion for Boxing led to this meeting of minds with James, and both expert-authors have constructed an exceptionally high-quality Kickboxing training manual.

Becoming a champion in combat sports is not for everyone. Becoming an international

Kickboxing champion is the privilege of a small minority, including James Turner.

James fights in the right way. He relies on technique, precision timing and great physical performance. The road to success in Full Contact Kickboxing includes blood, sweat and tears. Sacrifice must become your travel companion, a presence that never leaves you. Alongside physical and athletic ability, a fighter needs additional qualities in order to separate from the pack and aim high. James has all of these qualities. He will soon fulfil his dream of lifting the World Championship belt in an amazing performance.

Massimo Brizi
World Champion
IKTA Italia/Vice World President

PREFACE

ANDY DUMAS

Over the years, I have been asked the same question many times: 'Why do you participate in the art of fighting?' My answer is that Kickboxing is not fighting. Kickboxing is a sport. These athletes do not carry rage or anger into the ring. Inherent conflict is not present among competitive Kickboxers. They dedicate themselves to mastering the mental and physical aspects of the art of Kickboxing. They have a respect for themselves and their opponents.

This book is for all those interested in Kickboxing principles, from amateur Kickboxers to professionals, from Boxers to Martial Artists. The following chapters will guide you through all aspects of Kickboxing training. However, this book is not intended to replace the guidance and supervision of an experienced coach, rather to complement a coach's instruction. As a dedicated athlete, you must train with the mindset that every opponent will be superior. To put it simply: prepared, educated and informed Kickboxers make better choices in the ring and in training. *Full Contact Kickboxing – A Complete Guide to Training and Strategies* is the most comprehensive and complete examination and review of the sport and discipline of Kickboxing that has been published to date. It has been a privilege to have as my co-author James 'The Dragon' Turner, accomplished Kickboxing Champion and Hall of Fame Martial Artist.

Andy Dumas.

My boxing/fitness career has spanned several decades, and I have been fortunate to spend time with some of the greatest athletes to have ever laced up the gloves. However, there is no doubt that the pinnacle were the times I spent with my idol, the great Muhammad Ali, who inspired millions around the world to be the best that they can be.

I hope this book motivates and inspires you to be the best you can be.

JAMES TURNER

My Martial Arts journey began at a young age. Inspired by the great champions, I found my path: Kickboxing. I have experienced many inspirational moments during my time in the sport. I have taken great pleasure in hosting seminars by pioneering World Champion Bill 'Superfoot' Wallace in Cornwall, England.

In 2017, I was honoured to be asked by legendary World Champion Don 'The Dragon' Wilson to be in his corner for his 'Comeback' Exhibition Match. In 2019, I was bestowed with the honour of being appointed IKTA UK/Great Britain President by legendary World Champion Massimo Brizi. And in 2020, I was honoured to be invited by my favourite Boxing training author, Andy Dumas, to co-author the book you are reading now. In 2021 and 2022, I was recognized in the UK Black Belt Hall Of Fame, having been recognized in the UK Martial Arts Hall Of Fame in 2018. All of these were humbling and inspirational moments in my life.

James 'The Dragon' Turner.

From a young age, I wanted to follow in the footsteps of those who inspired me. I still walk this path today; training to be the best Martial Artist that I can be. I was inspired to relish the training and dedication required to excel in the Martial Arts. I hope Andy and I can provide some meaningful inspiration for you.

WBC

INTRODUCTION TO THE 'SPORT OF KINGS'

THE BEGINNING

In the early 1970s, a Martial Arts phenomenon was emerging in the United States and the western hemisphere. Throughout the previous decade, the Martial Arts had received increasingly significant exposure and interest through movies, television, books, magazines and popular culture. Celebrities such as Sean Connery, Dean Martin, Steve McQueen and Elvis Presley were vocal about their interest and practice of the Martial Arts. Television shows such as *Kung Fu* starring David Carradine achieved massive popularity, and the young Martial Arts master and actor who was known to American audiences as Kato, the trusty chauffeur and 'sidekick' to The Green Hornet, had been starring in record breaking movies in Hong Kong, and was about to become a global superstar and icon with the release of the 1973 classic *Enter the Dragon*. That man was, of course, Bruce Lee.

While this rise in Martial Arts popularity was happening in the entertainment industry, the desire of the public to learn these skills was concurrently growing. Karate, Kung Fu, Tae Kwon Do and Judo schools were appearing across the United States throughout the 1960s, increasing the public's opportunity to learn Asian arts of self-defence. The striking-based styles – those concerned with punching and kicking – were generally marketed as forms of Karate. This Martial Arts uprising would carry across from the US to Canada, to South America, and across the pond to European countries and beyond.

Along with the recreational interest, Martial Arts-based sport flourished in the US. Karate tournaments were the proving ground for competitors of the 1960s and early 1970s. Known as Point Karate, Point Fighting, or Semi Contact, the sport features the use of traditional Karate techniques in a controlled manner, i.e. a punch or a kick is executed with restraint. If a technique is performed with excessive force, that would lead to penalties and potentially, eventual disqualification. Only one technique can score by either competitor before the referee halts the action to award a point to the scoring fighter. Point Karate is a great sport and requires a high level of skill, speed, timing and accuracy, but some of the top competitors of that era longed for a more dynamic and less restrictive form of Martial Arts competition.

OPPOSITE: James Turner and Andy Dumas.

One such competitor was World Heavyweight Karate Champion Joe Lewis, who as a US Marine stationed on the island of Okinawa, had learnt the art of Shorin-Ryu Karate. When he returned to the US he continued to develop and expand his Martial Arts repertoire during his competitive Karate career. He trained extensively in Boxing with former Heavyweight contender Joe Orbillo, and began working with then sought-after instructor Bruce Lee, who was interested in sharing his Jeet Kune Do fighting principles with the Karate competitor Lewis. Unlike many Martial Artists of the time period, Lee trained and taught with modern and innovative training apparatus such as the Boxing heavy bag, focus pads, the double-end-bag and football tackle shield for practising side kicks. These training approaches were concerned with realistic combat, punching and kicking with full force. This was not something that all Martial Artists or Martial Arts competitors at the time were concerned with gravitating towards. Some did, however.

Defeating the top competitors of the time, Lewis credited his time with Lee as one of the key factors that encouraged him to move in a new direction. Lewis and others, including promoter Mike Anderson, were determined to bring this approach into the limelight as a sport. Subsequently, Lewis fought some early matches; the first was against Greg Baines in 1970 where the ring announcer identified the fighters as 'Kickboxers'.

The sport of Full Contact Karate (now known as Kickboxing) officially began on 14 September 1974 at the Los Angeles Sports Arena, California, USA. The debut of the sport was highlighted on ABC's 'Wide World of Entertainment' and saw four World Champions crowned: Joe Lewis (Heavyweight, USA), Jeff Smith (Light Heavyweight, USA), Bill Wallace (Middleweight, USA) and Isaias Duenas (Lightweight, Mexico). The television broadcast attained the highest rating in its time slot for the previous two years. The sport became, as Bill 'Superfoot' Wallace described it, '... an overnight sensation. Everybody in the whole world wanted to do Full Contact Karate.' Audiences were enthralled by the exciting action on display; it was the first time that television viewers had seen top Martial Arts athletes compete against each other using maximum force – literally, Full Contact.

Bill 'Superfoot' Wallace.

The 14 September 1974 event marked the beginning of Professional Martial Arts Fighting as a sport in North America, leading to the growth and development of what would become known as Kickboxing. Pioneering leaders in the sport such as Joe Corley and Howard Hanson developed their organizations through world rankings, television exposure and by establishing platforms for the superstars of the sport to flourish. Kickboxing paved the way for other combat sports to emerge from the Martial Arts boom of the '70s, '80s and '90s, including Mixed Martial Arts (MMA). Today, several combat sports allow their competitors to kick, whereas this was a novelty to western audiences in the 1970s when Kickboxing debuted on television. Until that point in time, western television audiences only knew Professional Boxing as 'the' sport where competitors fought to the knockout.

WHAT'S IN A NAME?

When someone asks about the term Full Contact Kickboxing, the simplest explanation would be that the name refers to the top designation of the sport, the variations being Semi Contact, Light Contact and Full Contact Kickboxing. However, you may also come across the sport being referred to as Full Contact Karate, Contact Karate or American Kickboxing. In addition to this, you may observe 'Kickboxing' matches that have vastly different rules to those laid out in this book. Why?

The answer lies in the development of our sport at a time when other combat sports were also coming into the public consciousness.

As the 1970s progressed, the *then* named Full Contact Karate community became increasingly aware of the advantages of implementing offensive and defensive techniques from Boxing into their repertoire. While the first wave of champions already had Boxing training, increasing numbers of the top competitors that followed were hiring Boxing trainers and working out in Boxing gyms, either exclusively, or alongside training at their Karate Dojos. By the end of the 1970s, Point Karate gloves were replaced by boxing gloves, 'throwing' techniques were taken out of competition and the Boxing ring was now the standard fighting area for Full Contact Karate. This evolution of the fighting techniques and the rules contributed to the sport becoming widely known as Kickboxing. World Champion Benny 'The Jet' Urquidez recalls that he and his peers were already referring to the sport as Kickboxing in 1975.

As the sport continued into the 1980s, the terms Full Contact Karate and Kickboxing were often used interchangeably. Different organizations also used variations of these terms. When fighters were being introduced

Benny 'The Jet' Urquidez.

in the ring during the mid-to-late 1980s, it wasn't uncommon to hear their 'Contact Karate' or 'American Kickboxing' records being announced to the crowd.

By the 1990s, the term Kickboxing had been established to define the sport. The top champions were now commonly known as World Kickboxing Champions – more frequently so than Karate Champions. The sport had stars, and their profiles consolidated the term Kickboxing in the public consciousness. Don 'The Dragon' Wilson starred in over thirty successful Martial Arts action movies to complement his record-setting World Championship Kickboxing career. In the wake of Chuck Norris' *A Force of One* and some other early examples, Wilson's films pioneered 'Kickboxing movies' as their own sub-genre. *American Kickboxer* (1991) starring John Barrett and Keith Vitali and *Psycho Kickboxer* (1997) starring Curtis Bush further exemplified the establishment of the term 'Kickboxing'.

Within the combat sports world, into the 1990s and through to today, use of the term 'Full Contact' remains to distinguish the sport from other disciplines. This is because the term 'Kickboxing' has become something of an 'umbrella term' to describe various

Don 'The Dragon' Wilson.

different combat sports that prioritize kicking and punching techniques. These include Muay Thai/Thai Boxing (referred to by some as 'Muay Thai Kickboxing'), Sanda/San Shou (sometimes referred to as 'Chinese Kickboxing') as well as other formats such as K-1 Rules (referred to by some as 'K-1 Kickboxing') and International/Freestyle Rules Kickboxing (which include kicking to the legs). In the late 1950s, the term 'Kickboxing' was already being used in Japan to describe more brutal bouts in which fighters wore shorts, no shin or foot protection and used knee strikes in addition to kicks and punches. During the mid-to-late 1970s, 'Full Contact Karate' fighters fought against 'Japanese Kickboxers' in international matches, but it wasn't long before Full Contact Karate fighters became more widely known as Kickboxers themselves, including in Japan. Benny 'The Jet' Urquidez was the first American Full Contact Karate/Kickboxing athlete to become a favourite with Japanese fight fans. Being featured in a Japanese comic book series is just one example of his fame and impact as an early pioneer.

Because of the broad usage of the term 'Kickboxing' in various regions of the world and by numerous organizations, each sport/rule-set needs its own accompanying term to provide clarification. Therefore, Full Contact Kickboxing is used as a long-form title of our sport. This term serves not only to distinguish the discipline from other combat sports, but also of its own variants: Semi Contact, Light Contact and Full Contact Kickboxing. You may still come across the word Karate being used interchangeably with Kickboxing; this is a reflection of the sport's roots and its foundation in the traditional Martial Arts.

So, if someone asks you which martial art or combat sport you train or compete in, the easiest-to-understand answer you can give is Kickboxing. If they need clarification, you can tell them *Full Contact Kickboxing*!

The prestige of Full Contact Kickboxing

Full Contact Kickboxing demands the highest degree of technical skill, physical conditioning and cerebral discipline. While several sports today allow their competitors to kick, Full Contact Kickboxing can be easily distinguished by the newcomer to combat sports in several ways: while sports such as Muay Thai and MMA allow kicks to the legs of opponents, and knees to the body and head, Full Contact Kickboxers

Massimo 'The Iceman' Brizi.

must rely on their technical expertise by throwing all of their kicks above the waist (kicks below the waist are not allowed). Elbows, knees and grappling of any kind are also prohibited in Full Contact Kickboxing; the athlete must win the bout purely with kicking and punching, i.e. Kickboxing techniques.

This rules system demands a tremendous level of skill, conditioning and expertise that make Full Contact Kickboxing fights spectacular and exciting; the high kicks and combinations on display are not replicated with the same consistency in any other sport. There is not a more thrilling fight possible than when two world class Full Contact Kickboxers meet in the ring.

Full Contact Kickboxing mandates that competitors wear long Full Contact Kickboxing pants/trousers, which are indicative of the sport's roots in traditional Martial Arts. These long pants distinguish Kickboxing from Boxing, in which competitors wear shorts. The rules of Full Contact Kickboxing also protect the fighters from unnecessary injury; the sport respects its athletes and prioritizes their safety. Boxing gloves protect the fighter's hands from superficial skin and bone damage, as well as providing that protection to their opponent's head and body. It only stands to reason that the same provisions are taken with the legs. In some other combat sports, fighters wear gloves on their hands but no protective equipment on their feet or legs. This practice is unnecessarily dangerous to the athletes and looks incomplete from the viewer's perspective. This is why competition-regulation kick boots and shin guards are mandatory in Full Contact Kickboxing. The fighters' protective equipment on their hands, feet and shins – as well as the rules prohibiting brutal bone-on-bone contact such as elbow and knee strikes – enforces uniformity, safety and spectacular fighting that represents martial artistry and sportsmanship at the highest level.

Massimo Brizi in World Title fight.

The emergence of the various kick-punch fight sports in the public eye caused some dissention and 'style-vs.-style' arguments in the Martial Arts community. It has often been documented that in 1988, a young Rick Roufus (who went on to be regarded as one of the greatest Kickboxers of all time) was caught off-guard by the low leg-kicks of Muay Thai fighter Changpuek Kiatsongrit in a bout allowing 'low kicks' in Las Vegas, Nevada USA. Roufus went on to win World Championship bouts in International Rules and K-1 Rules matches that allowed low kicks, in addition to six World Titles in Full Contact Kickboxing, but he did suffer significant damage to his legs in the bout with Kiatsongrit in 1988. This bout is often cited as an endorsement for Muay Thai as a superior art/sport. However, those who endorse this sentiment tend to ignore (some perhaps are unaware) that American Full Contact Kickboxers such as Benny Urquidez and Don Wilson had defeated Muay Thai fighters during their careers, without being significantly impacted by their opponents' low kicks. This was *before* the Roufus vs. Kiatsongrit bout.

In the years since, a historically important bout took place in 2006 when Full Contact Kickboxing World Champion Massimo Brizi of Italy travelled to Thailand for a Muay Thai World Title bout. Brizi defeated his Thai opponent, Yodheca, and became Muay Thai World Champion. Full Contact Kickboxing and Muay Thai are both great arts; the individual fighters make the difference to the outcome of a bout. The style-vs-style arguments miss the point; Bruce Lee encouraged that Martial Artists utilize what works 'for them' from the various Martial Arts they study. He professed: 'Absorb what is useful, reject what is useless and add what is essentially your own.'

THE INTERCONTINENTAL KICK THAI BOXING ASSOCIATION (IKTA) FULL CONTACT RULES AND REGULATIONS

> *In IKTA Full Contact bouts, we showcase the martial artistry and thrilling action that are signatures of the sport, and we prioritize the safety of the athletes.*
>
> *Massimo Brizi,*
> *World Champion, IKTA Italia/Vice World President*

The Intercontinental Kick Thai Boxing Association (IKTA) is an international combat sports federation that promotes and organizes combat sports events such as Kickboxing and Muay Thai. Founded in 2012 in Mexico (President Marco Ghibaudo), branches were subsequently created in South America, Asia, Africa and Europe. Co-author James Turner is one of four Black Belts personally certified by Full Contact World Champion and IKTA Italia/Vice World President, Massimo Brizi. In the United Kingdom, James represents the IKTA as its Great Britain President, as well as being an international supervisor for the association.

IKTA.

James Turner and Massimo Brizi.

Fighters' attire/equipment

Fighters wear Full Contact Kickboxing long pants, boxing gloves, kick boots, shin guards, groin guards and mouthpieces. Male competitors are bare torso while female competitors wear sports bras/chest protectors.

Legal techniques

All Boxing techniques are permitted along with all kicking techniques above the waist and sweeps that are boot-to-boot only. Punches and kicks are to be aimed to the front and sides of the head and body.

Illegal techniques

Kicks below the waist, grabbing or holding the leg, knee strikes, elbow strikes, headbutts, and striking the groin, the back or the back of the head are all illegal manoeuvres. As in the case of Professional Boxing, holding and hitting of

Andrea 'The Snake' Rinaldi.

any kind is illegal; both hands must be free when executing all techniques.

Fighters' obligations in the ring

Each fighter must perform only legal techniques with the intention to land the techniques on the legal targets on their opponent's head and body. Each fighter must make a sincere effort to attempt to land six kicks per round, or they will automatically lose the round. Each fighter must pay attention to and follow the instructions of the referee at all times.

Rounds

Rounds are 2 minutes in duration with 1-minute rest periods between each round.

National Title Fights: five rounds
International Title Fights: five rounds
Continental Title Fights: seven rounds
Intercontinental Title Fights: seven rounds
World Title Fights: nine rounds

Alessio 'Angel Face' Crescentini.

Stress and trauma physicians have measured that performing nine 2-minute rounds of Full Contact Kickboxing is equal to the energy expenditure required to complete fifteen 3-minute rounds of Professional Boxing. This can be attributed to the requirement to throw a minimum number of kicks, all above the waist, per round.

Scoring

Scoring is based on the following categories: effective offensive techniques, effective defensive techniques, effective aggression, and ring generalship.

- Effective offensive techniques: punches and kicks scoring cleanly on the front or sides of the opponent's head or body; punches and kicks that land on the gloves or arms do not count.
- Effective defensive techniques: parrying, blocking, slipping, weaving and footwork. Continual avoidance of contact and repeatedly showing unwillingness to fight does not count, and could lead to point deductions and eventual disqualification.
- Effective aggression: effectively moving towards the opponent and using this

aggression to set up effective offensive techniques.

- Ring generalship: effectively controlling the ring, whether offensively or defensively, in order to set up effective offensive techniques. A defensive footwork strategy can be utilized to counter an opponent's aggressive strategy and will be recognized in the scoring if the fighter is able to execute effective offensive techniques, and defensive techniques if necessary, against their aggressive opponent. The fighter with superior ring generalship is the one who controls the fight.

Three judges at ringside score each round on a 10-point must system: the winner of each round scores 10 points; the loser scores 9 points or less, based on the level of superiority of the winner of the round. A knockdown automatically results in the deduction of a point from the fighter who was knocked down. If the winner of the round does not knock his opponent down, he will win the round 10–9. If the winner of the round knocks his opponent down once, or significantly dominates his opponent without scoring a knockdown, he will win the round 10–8. If the winner of the round knocks his opponent down twice, he will win the round 10–7, and so on.

If the bout is completed to the full scheduled duration without a knockout, the scores for each round by each of the three judges will be tallied, and the weight of majority determines the result.

For example, after nine rounds of fighting, if the three judges return scores of:

Judge 1: 90–81, Judge 2: 89–82 and Judge 3: 90–81, Fighter A wins by unanimous decision.

If the judges return scores of:

Judge 1: 85–84, Judge 2: 84–86 and Judge 3: 84–85, Fighter B wins by split decision.

The IKTA utilizes odd numbers of rounds, such as five, seven and nine rounds for bouts. This decreases the likelihood of a draw occurring, a situation where neither fighter scores more points than the other, preventing a winner from being declared. This is because it is less likely that the fighters can share a number of rounds won throughout the duration of a contest, such as in a fight with an even number of rounds. For example, if a bout was scheduled for eight rounds, and each fighter won four rounds, by scores of 10–9 in every round, the result would be a draw. If the same bout was scheduled for nine rounds, it is likely that one of the two fighters would win the ninth round. This means that one fighter will have won five rounds to four, thus allowing a winner to be decided.

In the less likely event of a draw occurring in an odd-numbered-rounds contest, these are examples of how it could occur:

If the judges return scores of:

Judge 1: 85–85, Judge 2: 84–84 and Judge 3: 85–85, the result is a draw.

If the judges return scores of:

Judge 1: 85–85, Judge 2: 85–85 and Judge 3: 87–84, the result is a majority draw.

If the judges return scores of:

Judge 1: 85–84, Judge 2: 84–85 and Judge 3: 85–85, the result is a split draw.

For these draw results to occur, one or both fighters would ordinarily need to have knocked the other down, or to have dominated the other for periods of the fight, but also losing rounds in the process. Another possibility is that points would have been deducted due to fouls. Essentially, it requires a more complex situation for a draw to occur in an odd-numbered-rounds contest than in an even-numbered-rounds contest, where a competitive fight could result in both fighters winning 50 per cent of the bout by 10–9 scores. An odd-numbered-rounds contest prevents this situation from occurring, and the IKTA's round system encourages that a winner is determined in each bout.

WEIGHT DIVISIONS

WEIGHT DIVISIONS
57kg/125.66lbs
61kg/134.48lbs
64kg/141.09lbs
67kg/147.71lbs
70kg/154.32lbs
73kg/160.93lbs
76kg/167.55lbs
80kg/176.37lbs
85kg/187.39lbs
90kg/198.41lbs
90kg+

In Title Fights, there is a 0.5kg allowance above the limit of each designated weight division. If a fighter 'misses weight' (weighs more than the allowance), then there are three options/possibilities:

1. The fighter does not compete and their opponent wins automatically.

If the fighter *does* choose to compete, the opponent can choose a stipulation:

2. The fighter agrees to compete with the acceptance of a monetary fine.

   or

3. The fighter agrees to compete with the stipulation that their opponent automatically wins a round for each additional kg weighed in. For example, if the fighter was 3kg overweight, the opponent has already won the first three rounds before the bout begins. Scoring would therefore start from the fourth round, in this example.

KICKBOXING BELT RANKINGS

This system of coloured belt rankings is as prescribed by Master Massimo Brizi, IKTA Italia/Vice World President. In addition to his legendary fighting career, winning twenty-two Professional World Title Fights, Master Brizi has been an innovator of the sport. As well as promoting international IKTA fight events, he has pioneered a comprehensive grading system that ensures IKTA Kickboxing students ascend in rank according to technical proficiency, practical experience

James Turner, Massimo Brizi and Alessio Crescentini.

and psychological maturity. Instructors in Italy, England and the United States follow this official grading system:

Yellow belt
Orange belt
Green belt
Blue belt
Brown belt
Black belt

Upon attaining 1st Degree Black Belt, the Kickboxer continues to ascend through grading tests, with the highest level being 10th Degree. To attain such a Degree would require decades of training, commitment, dedication and time served to the sport and art of Kickboxing.

IKTA

2 KICKBOXING FUNDAMENTALS

Properly mastering the fundamentals is vital to success in any activity, game or sport, and there is no exception in Kickboxing training. To develop and master the Kickboxing fundamentals, consistently train with focus and purpose. This will create a stable base for you to build upon, allowing for your fitness level and skills to progress naturally. When developing new skills, aim to make them a habit. A habit is a conditioned reflex that is the result of repetitive movements. The goal is to practise the fundamental skills until they become 'good' habits.

Orthodox stance.

THE CLASSIC STANCE

All moves in Kickboxing originate from a balanced stance. It is the foundation of smooth, steady movement that facilitates the delivery of effective kicks and punch combinations. It is essential that you develop a kickboxing stance that provides stability and allows you to move easily.

Finding the right stance for you

Traditionally, your stance corresponds to your dominant hand. If your dominant hand is your right hand, you would adopt an 'orthodox' stance. The left shoulder and the left foot are forward, allowing for the easy execution of the left jab. Developing a solid jab will allow you to set up power punches such as the rear straight

OPPOSITE: Kickboxing fundamentals.

punch, known as the cross. If your dominant hand is your left hand, then the right shoulder and right foot are forward, and you will utilize a right jab. This is referred to as the 'southpaw' stance.

Throughout the history of Kickboxing, most fighters have abided by this system of putting their dominant hand to the rear, as in Boxing. However, some of the top champions in both Boxing and Kickboxing prefer to fight with the dominant hand in the lead position, as they find this to be more comfortable and effective for them. For example, Bill 'Superfoot' Wallace was a left-handed orthodox fighter, and retired undefeated as World Champion. The important point is to find the stance that is most natural to you. This can take time and experience to discover, so if you're unsure, it is recommended that you stay with the traditional method as described previously: orthodox stance for right-handers and southpaw stance for left-handers.

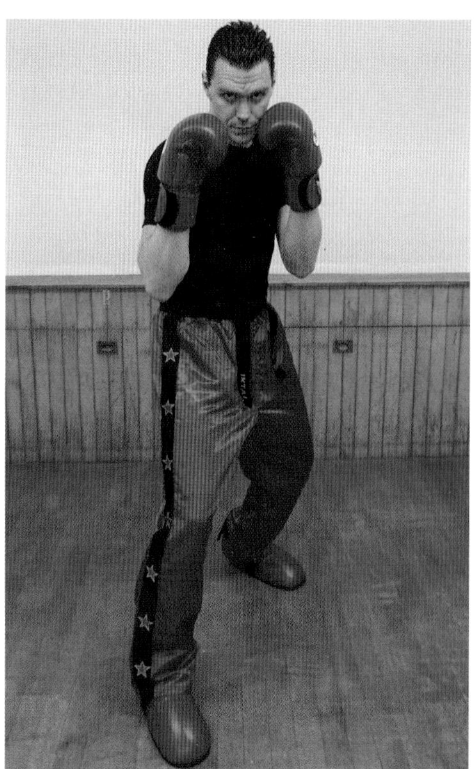

Southpaw stance.

Throughout this book, Andy will demonstrate his moves and combinations from the orthodox stance, while James will perform his from the southpaw stance. This will help train you to identify specific moves, regardless of the stance they're performed in. You will be able to recognize techniques as, for example, a 'lead hook' or a 'rear roundhouse kick' (rather than a 'left hook' or a 'right roundhouse kick'). Being able to make distinctions like these will elevate your understanding of Kickboxing.

Feet and legs

Proper foot placement is one of the most important elements for an effective Kickboxing stance.

If your foot placement is incorrect, your movement will be ineffective and inefficient when shadowboxing, working the heavy bags or working on the focus pads. Your feet should point approximately at a 45-degree angle to the side when facing your opponent.

It is essential to start with a solid base to execute all moves. Stand with your feet shoulder width apart or slightly wider. Step backward with your right or left foot depending on your fighting stance. When facing your opponent, the heel of your back or rear foot should approximately line up with the toe of your front or lead foot. This toe-to-heel line can vary by a few inches, depending on your body structure and what's comfortable. Equally distribute your body weight between the lead and rear feet. If too much weight is placed on your lead foot, it makes it difficult to step away quickly after you have thrown a punch. It also reduces the ability to pivot on the rear foot and decreases the power behind your cross. Centre your body weight through the balls of your feet, with the heel of the rear foot slightly raised. The raised back heel allows you to move and respond quickly. Your lower body position should feel balanced and allow for easy movement in all directions. Keep your knees slightly bent allowing for better mobility, power, and a balanced movement. Do not bend your knees too much, as this will result in clumsy and sluggish movement.

The body

Your upper body is positioned at a 45-degree angle providing leverage while minimizing your own target area. Your front shoulder, front hip, and forward foot line up. Keep your abdominals firm, and your shoulders slightly rounded, forward, and relaxed. Focus on the centre of your body and start all your movements from deep within your core. The power of your punch is generated from a strong, centred core.

The arms and shoulders

Hold your arms close to the sides of the body by the ribcage, with your shoulders relaxed and slightly rounded. The elbows are bent and pointing down and in, thereby protecting your ribcage and solar plexus. Keep both hands up by your face. Kickboxers are constantly adjusting the position of their arms in order to defend against various punches and kicks to the head and body from their opponents.

The hands and fists

Keep your fists up high, in the 'on-guard position'. This is the best position to deliver your punches. Close your fingers together to make a loose fist, with your thumb folding to the outside of the fingers and do not clench your fist too tight. Turn your fists inward slightly and keep your wrists straight and strong. The Kickboxer often holds the rear fist slightly higher, very close to the chin, and the lead fist held just above the top of the lead shoulder. It is from this position that all punches are executed. Your fists are always in the 'on-guard position' unless you are throwing a punch.

The head

Keep your eyes in the direction of the target (the various punching bags or focus pads). Your chin stays tucked in towards your chest and your head slightly forward and down. Once again, these movements are replicating the strategies of a Kickboxer. This is the head space you need to be in when performing your workouts.

Keys to Success

- Keep your legs and feet in a balanced stance, ready to move.
- Point the toes of your front/lead foot and back/rear foot out slightly to the side.
- Ensure your body weight is equally centred through the balls of your feet.
- Your rear foot is shoulder-width (or more) behind and its heel is lined up with the toe of your lead foot.
- Your abdominal core muscles are contracted and held firm when you're in close range or 'on the inside'.
- Keep your neck and shoulder muscles relaxed, allowing for easier execution of the punches.
- Stay on the balls of your feet with slightly bent knees. This allows for quick and efficient movement from one position to the next.
- Your front shoulder, hip, and foot are aligned and your body angles towards the target.
- Your arms are held close to the sides of the body with your elbows positioned by the rib cage.
- Close your fingers in a loose fist, with your thumb resting over the top of the fingers.
- Your fists turn in slightly and are held high in the 'on-guard' position.

PUNCHING TECHNIQUES

It is important to develop a multitude of smooth and technically correct single punches before working on punch combinations. Proper execution of each single punch must be duplicated over and over in order to improve your skills. Practise with purpose and stay focused on throwing one effective punch at a time. Your muscles need to be trained to react quickly and simultaneously in order to produce effective punches. The basic punches that need to be mastered are the jab, the cross, hooks, and uppercuts.

The jab

A fast, effective jab can be one of the most effective weapons for a Kickboxer. It sets up more powerful punches such as crosses, hooks and uppercuts. Throw the jab with speed, and accuracy. During any given round, whether shadowboxing or on the heavy bag, a multitude of jabs should be thrown continually.

Orthodox jab.

In a Kickboxing match the jab is the most frequently thrown punch in your arsenal (about 65 to 70 per cent of the total punches thrown) and can be utilized as both an offensive and defensive weapon.

Stand in your orthodox or southpaw stance, with your lead hand in a relaxed fist. Your lead arm snaps away from your body in a straight line towards the target. As your arm extends forward, your fist rotates and your palm faces down at point of impact. Fully extend your arm without any hyperextension at your elbow joint. Your shoulder follows through to protect your chin. When you launch the jab do not rotate your fist too early. Allow the rotation to flow from the movement that starts from your shoulder, extends through your elbow and then to your fist. Avoid the 'chicken wing' effect. This is when your elbow leaves the side of the body creating a sloppy and ineffective punch. This makes the punch powerless and ineffective.

After striking your target, bring your lead arm back to the on-guard position quickly and along the same path of the delivery. Protect your ribs by keeping your elbows close to the sides of your body. Remember to keep your rear hand by your face when throwing the jab.

Throw jabs to an opponent's head or body. When throwing punches to the body, bend your knees, thereby lowering the position of your punch. This is far more effective than dropping your hands. Practise this when shadowboxing or training on the heavy bag.

Once the effectiveness and the timing of your punch improves, increase your punch power by moving forward slightly as you launch your jab. To accomplish this, push off the ball of your back foot slightly and slide your front foot forward at the same time as you throw the punch. Your foot movement must be synchronized with your punch. Always execute your jab from a well-balanced position and breathe naturally, exhaling as you launch your punch. Get in the habit of throwing fast, quick jabs. This is also referred to as 'snapping your punches'. To deliver a snapping punch, throw quickly having minimal contact time with the target and then return straightaway to the on-guard position.

The main purpose of the jab is to keep your opponent at a safe distance, distracted, and off-guard. Get in the habit of throwing crisp jabs at different angles while moving around the target.

Keys to Success

- Elbow moves straight forward as you execute your jab. Do not lift it out sideways.
- Winding-up or pulling back the fist is another common mistake. Practise in front of a mirror to ensure your jab is thrown straight out and returns straight back to the on-guard position.
- Rotate your fist during the last third of the punch so your palm is facing down on impact. Focus on fully extending your arm and rotating your fist.
- Throw plenty of fast, snappy, crisp jabs.

The cross

The cross, similar to the reverse punch in Martial Arts circles, is a power punch executed with the rear hand. The cross takes more time and more energy to execute than the jab.

Starting in the on-guard stance, your rear hand is thrown from the chin as your rear shoulder thrusts forward. The fist travels in a straight line towards the target and rotates during the last third of the punch with your palm facing down. Power is generated from your trail foot and the punch travels straight forward to the target.

Orthodox cross.

Keep your core muscles tight to maintain correct alignment and a strong centre of balance. Remain on the balls of your feet with your rear hip rotating forward as you launch your cross. This simultaneous rotation of the rear hip and shoulder, along with the push from the ball of your rear foot, combine to produce a powerful cross.

Keep your lead hand in front of the face, ready to throw a follow-up punch. As with the jab, ensure that you do not pull the arm or lift your rear elbow before throwing the punch. Finish the punch with your hips square to the target, your chin down, and both eyes on the target. Swiftly return to the on-guard position as you prepare to throw your next punch. More muscles are engaged and more energy is required when throwing crosses.

Keys to Success

- The punch is a synchronized body movement, with your knees slightly bent for easy rotation of your torso, shoulders and hip regions.
- Make sure your shoulders and hips move together and your body weight is transferred from your back foot to your front foot when the punch is launched.
- Execute the punch in a straight line to the target. Do not lift your rear elbow.
- Stay up on the ball of your rear foot as you launch the punch.
- The lead (jab) fist remains in the on-guard position. Do not let it drop as you execute the cross.

Orthodox lead hook.

Hooks

The hook is a short-range, semi-circular punch most often thrown with your lead hand. The strength and velocity of this punch come from the synchronization of the body pivoting while rotating through the hips and pressing through the feet. In order for hooks to be effective, they must be thrown at close range. It is not a wild punch, but rather a punch thrown with precision and control.

The lead hook

With your hands in the on-guard position and your core muscles held tight, keep your knees slightly bent and your body weight centred through both of your legs. As you launch the punch, your lead elbow lifts away from the rib cage and the underside of your arm is parallel to the floor. The elbow is kept at a 90-degree angle throughout the delivery. Your shoulders and hips rotate clockwise and your lead foot pivots inward on the ball of your foot. Your wrist remains strong and your thumb points up allowing your knuckles to make solid contact. Quickly return your lead elbow to the side of the body and your lead fist up to protect the chin.

One advantage of an effective lead hook is the short distance it travels to reach the target.

The lead hook moves about one-third of the distance of the cross, making it a very deceptive punch. The hook can be delivered to the body or the head. Bending your knees and lowering your body puts you in the ideal position to land hooks to the body.

The rear hook

The rear hook comes from your rear hand and has to travel further. Pivot on the ball of your rear foot, quickly rotating your rear arm, shoulder, body, and hips in one movement in a counter-clockwise direction. The rear hook has a greater distance to travel to make contact. Your body moves the same way as when you throw a cross but your rear arm swings in a tight circular motion. You must step in closer to your target, as your arm is not extended fully. After the punch is thrown, quickly return to the

Orthodox rear hook.

on-guard position, fists up by your chin and elbows protecting your body.

The rear hook is not utilized as much as the lead hook in a Kickboxing match since the opponent can easily detect the wide-hooking motion coming off of the back foot. When working the heavy bag, a flurry of short left and right hooks to the body can be thrown at close range.

Keys to Success

- Keep your elbow bent at 90 degrees and at shoulder level.
- Move your arm and body as one unit and pivot on the balls of your feet.
- Move in and launch your punch when you are close to the target. A common mistake is to launch the punch when you are too far away from your target.
- Throw short, compact hooks. Do not throw big, looping hooks.

Uppercuts

Uppercuts are powerful, close-range punches and can be thrown by either the left or the right hand. The punch travels in an upward arc motion towards the target. Like the hook, this punch is considered an inside punch and you must be close to the target. Uppercuts can be delivered to your opponent's body or the chin.

The lead uppercut

The lead uppercut is thrown by positioning your body in a semi-crouching position to your lead side, with your lead shoulder lowered and your body weight transferring to the ball of your lead foot upon delivery of the punch. Keep the punch motion tight, using an upward driving force from your hips and legs to increase the power of the punch on impact. An uppercut thrown from a long range will lose some of its power because the arm is no longer sufficiently bent at the elbow and the total body's force will not be transferred in the upward movement. Learn to set up your uppercuts with straight punches (jabs and crosses) by moving in close to your target and launching them at close range.

Orthodox lead uppercut.

The rear uppercut

Orthodox rear uppercut.

To launch the rear uppercut, start in the on-guard position, keeping your rear knee relaxed with a slight bend. Your rear shoulder lowers to the rear side of the body and the lead fist stays high by your chin and head for protection. From this semi-crouching position, rotate your hips forward, throwing your fist upward in a rising arc towards the target. Your arm remains bent at the elbow, your wrist stays strong, and your rear shoulder follows through with the rotating hips. Upon impact, square your hips front and keep your elbows bent at a right angle. All of this occurs simultaneously in one smooth movement. Return to the on-guard position as quickly as possible, ready for the next move.

If you Kickbox in a southpaw stance, all your punches (and kicks) are the same techniques but 'mirrored' from the orthodox stance. For example, a southpaw fighter jabs with the right hand, while an orthodox fighter jabs with the left hand, etc.

Southpaw jab.

Southpaw cross.

1. Southpaw lead hook.

2. Southpaw rear hook.

3. Southpaw lead uppercut.

4. Southpaw rear uppercut.

KEYS TO SUCCESS

- Do not wind up or pull your arm back before throwing an uppercut.
- At the time of delivery and follow through, your elbow remains bent at a 90-degree angle for the most impact.
- Use the power and strength behind your body by transferring your weight forward and in the direction of your punch.
- Drive off the balls of your feet in order to execute the uppercut.
- Do not lean backward onto your heel.
- Keep your balance centred, with your core muscles held tight.

There are dozens of different ways to throw each punch depending on your body position, the timing of the punch execution, your body build, and individual idiosyncrasies. You can develop your own unique style of punching.

KICKING TECHNIQUES

One of the defining characteristics of Full Contact Kickboxing is the great kicking ability of its athletes. Unlike other fighting sports, Full Contact distinguishes itself by mandating that athletes target all attempted kicks above their opponent's waist, just as all punches must be aimed within the same parameters. Additionally, IKTA Full Contact athletes must attempt a minimum of six kicks per 2-minute round; lacklustre attempts to kick will not be recognized by the judges. These rules dictate that the fighters must possess a supreme level of skill, dexterity, precision and endurance. This is exemplified by a particular hallmark of the exceptional Full Contact Kickboxer: the ability to 'Box with your feet'. The highest level of offensive Kickboxing skill is the ability to utilize kicks and punches in combinations with equal effectiveness.

Fundamental kicks.

As when throwing punches, it is important to first develop technical proficiency with each individual kick in order to utilize them effectively and in combinations. Using proper form, execute your techniques with focus, precision, and speed. By studying the kicks in this guide, and with regular training, you will learn to throw your kicks as offensive, defensive and counter-offensive techniques. Well trained kickers can use their kicks as powerful weapons, as distractions to set up further techniques and as instantaneous reactions to particular situations in the ring.

As with punches, execute your kicking techniques with speed, accuracy and attention to defence. As fast as a kick is executed, the kicking leg must be returned to the ready position in the same manner. If executed recklessly, kicks can leave you very vulnerable to counter-attacks. You should follow the same fundamental defensive principles when kicking as when punching: keep your hands up, your chin down and your eyes on your opponent. Whichever kick or series of kicks you perform, ensure that you are able to finish in a defensively-responsible position.

Well-executed kicks are extremely powerful, and an accurately placed kick to the body or the head can instantly end a fight. Because your legs are larger than your arms, kicks are also more draining of your stamina, and if not well set-up, can be easier to see coming than punches. So, throw your kicks wisely and 'mix them up'. This is in order to make your opponent unsure of what's coming next. Several of these kicks require a 'chamber' which means to raise the kicking leg into position before launching the kick.

Front kick

If you have Martial Arts experience, it is likely that the first kick you were taught is the front kick. The most basic kick to perform, the front kick can be executed with the lead or rear leg. The power of the front kick is generated by thrusting your hips towards your opponent as you kick.

To throw the lead leg front kick, raise (chamber) your knee and then thrust your foot towards your target. The front kick is usually landed with the ball of the foot, but if you are flexible enough, you can land it with the heel instead; both parts of the foot are effective. To increase the power of your kick, move forward with the kick. To do this, push off the ball of your back foot and kick with your front foot at the same time. This creates the same dynamic as moving forward with the jab. Always throw your front kick from a well-balanced position

1. Stance.

Front kick chambered.

2. Lead front kick chambered.

3. Lead front kick extended.

1. Rear front kick chambered.

and breathe naturally; exhale as you launch your kick.

The rear leg front kick is thrown in the same fashion. Your kick will have to travel further, and your upper body will be more 'squared on' with your opponent, so keep your fists to your face and your elbows to your body to protect your now larger target area. After the kick, be sure to immediately return your kicking foot to its starting position and assume your fighting stance.

Front kicks, like straight punches, can be used for different reasons. For example: to set up techniques, to serve as a distraction, to create distance, or to cause significant damage by itself. While front kicks are most often thrown to the body, fighters have knocked their opponents out with front kicks to the face. A front kick can be thrown as a quick snapping kick, or as a hard thrusting kick with full force.

When throwing the front kick, be sure to maintain proper position: hands up, chin down and elbows in, protecting the body. Kicking, in general, can lead to countering opportunities against you. However, if you throw your

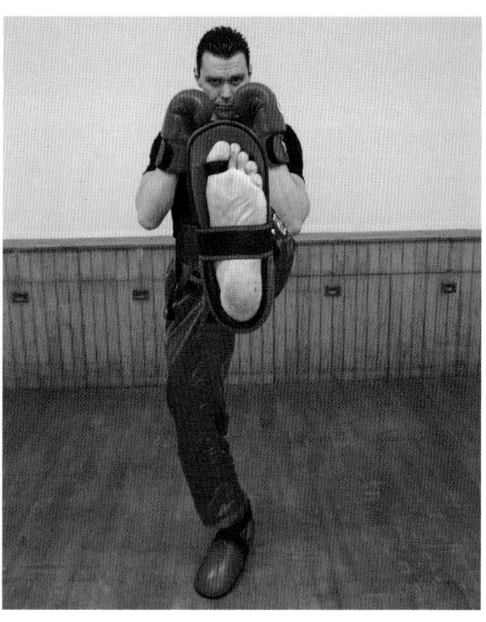

2. Rear front kick extended.

1. Stance.

2. Rear front kick chambered.

3. Rear front kick extended.

kicks while maintaining the proper upper body defensive position, particularly in the case of the front kick, then your kicks can be great strategic weapons. It can be very difficult to land jabs and straight punches on someone who keeps their hands up and throws front kicks into the body.

Keys to Success

- The front kick shoots directly towards your opponent in a straight line. Do not implement any circular motion to this kick.
- Telegraphing this kick is a common issue; avoid lifting the arms above the head before throwing the kick.
- Practise in front of a mirror to ensure your front kick is thrown straight out and returning straight back to the on-guard position.
- Make contact with the ball of the foot or the heel, making sure to curl your toes back to avoid injury.
- Fully extend the kick but avoid 'locking out' at the knee.
- Keep your fists up by your face and your elbows in by your ribcage when throwing the kick.

Roundhouse kick

When in front of your opponent in your fighting stance, the 'roundhouse' or 'round' kick travels around the side, landing on either side of your opponent's head or body.

Roundhouse kick.

The lead leg roundhouse kick

There are variations of how to throw a roundhouse with the lead leg. It can be thrown as a fast, snapping kick that is difficult to see coming at all, or as a powerful knockout kick with maximal body rotation.

The 'jabbing' type roundhouse is great for stunning your opponent and setting up subsequent attacks. Initiate the kick by raising your leg into a cocked-knee chamber. From this position, snap the roundhouse kick out and back as fast as possible, almost like a whip, making contact with the instep or shin, depending on the distance between you and your opponent. The kick can be targeted to the head or the body, and can be used while stationary, advancing or retreating. To throw the kick while advancing, in the same fashion as the front kick, push off the ball of your back foot with control and kick forward with your front foot at the same time. Your support foot will turn so your heel is pointed towards your opponent.

1. Stance.

2. Lead roundhouse kick chambered.

3. Lead roundhouse kick extended.

1. Stance.

The 'power' lead leg roundhouse is fundamentally the same kick, but with more rotation of the support foot, hips and shoulders. From your fighting stance, start pivoting your support foot and rotate your kicking leg towards your target. At the moment of impact, quickly rotate fully on your support foot while you twist your hips and shoulders vigorously into the direction of the kick, driving your kick into your target and making contact with the instep or shin, depending on the distance between you and your opponent. Your lower leg should be parallel to the floor on impact. To throw this kick while advancing, slide your rear foot towards your lead foot before initiating the kick. It is wise to disguise this footwork method with a jab, a feint or a punch combination while sliding your support foot forward.

A variation of the roundhouse kick involves kicking the target with the ball of the foot instead of the instep or lower shin. This is a useful tactical variation when used with the lead leg, as the quick-jabbing nature of the kick can start to dig into the opponent's ribs and

2. Slide-step.

3. Lead roundhouse kick chambered.

4. Lead roundhouse kick extended.

take their toll over the course of several rounds. A quick ball-of-the-foot roundhouse can also be a damaging kick to the face, particularly against an opponent who stands 'square' or has a wide guard position.

The rear leg roundhouse kick

This is one of the most powerful kicks you can throw because of the rotational force generated as the kick travels towards its target.

1. Rear roundhouse kick chambered.

2. Rear roundhouse kick extended.

From your fighting stance, start pivoting your support foot and rotate your kicking leg towards your target. At the moment of impact, quickly rotate fully on your support foot while you twist your hips and shoulders vigorously into the direction of the kick, driving your kick into your target and making contact with the instep or shin, depending on the distance between you and your opponent. Your lower leg should be parallel to the floor on impact. To throw this kick while advancing, take a step forward with your lead foot prior to kicking; your toes should point at 11 o'clock if you're orthodox and 1 o'clock if you're southpaw. From that position, start pivoting your lead foot and complete the kick from there.

Roundhouse kicks are thrown frequently in Kickboxing competitions because of their versatility and effectiveness. When throwing the roundhouse kick, be sure to maintain proper position: hands up, chin down and elbows in, protecting the body.

Keys to Success

- The roundhouse kick comes 'around'. Make sure to correctly aim the kick around the opponent's guard.
- Concentrate on rotating the ball of the support foot, the hips and the shoulders to generate power with the roundhouse kick.
- Avoid elaborate steps and 'wavy' arm movements before launching the kick – a common mistake.
- Stay up on *and rotate on* the ball of your support foot as you throw a powerful roundhouse kick.
- 'Mix it up' between throwing roundhouse kicks to the body and to the head.
- Keep your hands up, your chin down and your eyes on your opponent when executing roundhouse kicks.

The side kick

The side kick travels in a straight line towards the opponent and contact is made with the bottom of the heel. Landing this kick with the whole foot dissipates its power, so train yourself to hit with the heel as much as possible when throwing side kicks. The side kick is usually thrown with the lead leg, although a rear leg side kick can be a deceptive and powerful technique. To perform a rear leg side kick, your leg will have to travel across your body in order to chamber it in the same way as with the lead leg side kick. This makes the rear leg side kick take longer, but it can be a deceptive weapon, such as when the opponent may be anticipating a rear leg roundhouse kick; their defence will be focused in the wrong direction. The focus of this instructional guide is

Side kick.

on the lead leg side kick, as this is an essential technique in your arsenal.

> *My lead leg side kick is my strongest technique. And everything I do – hook, jab, roundhouse kick, cross – all comes from that platform.*
>
> *Don 'The Dragon' Wilson, World Champion*

As one of the most effective techniques you can throw, the lead leg side kick should be used frequently. A hard side kick to the body can completely take the wind out of your opponent. When their attention is on their body, this is a great time to follow up with a side kick to the head. Throw the lead leg side kick like your jab; using this kick in succession can drive an opponent across the ring and set up other techniques.

To perform the lead leg side kick, raise your leg into a cocked-knee chamber whilst pointing the bottom of your heel at your opponent. From this position, thrust your heel directly towards your target. It is important to pivot on the ball of your supporting foot so that the back of its heel is pointed towards your opponent as your side kick lands. This pivot allows the muscles of your hips, glutes and thighs to get

2. Lead side kick chambered.

1. Stance.

3. Lead side kick extended.

behind the kick. Return your leg to your stance following the same path as when throwing the kick. To move forward with the side kick, push off the ball of your back foot and kick with your front foot at the same time. This creates the same dynamic as moving forward with the jab. You can also slide-step to advance while throwing the lead leg side kick, i.e. sliding the rear foot towards your lead foot before initiating the kick. Always throw your side kick from a well-balanced position and breathe naturally; exhale as you launch your kick.

When kicking high with the side kick, follow all the same principles as when kicking to the body; always keeping your hands up, chin down and elbows in, protecting the body.

Hook kick.

Keys to Success

- Chamber the knee and shoot the side kick directly towards your opponent in a straight line.
- Twist your hips and shoulders, pointing your support foot in the opposite direction.
- Practise in front of a mirror to ensure your side kick is thrown straight out and returns straight back to the on-guard position.
- Make contact with the heel; do not try to strike with the whole foot or the ball of the foot.
- Fully extend the kick but avoid 'locking out' at the knee.
- Keep your fists up by your face and your elbows in by your ribcage when throwing the kick.
- Throw the lead leg side kick frequently, like a jab.

The hook kick

The hook kick can be considered a variation of the side kick that 'hooks' around to the side of the opponent's face. The hook kick is particularly effective when thrown to the head; you will seldom see a professional Kickboxer attempt a hook kick to the body. Like the side kick, it is a difficult kick to defend against when thrown with the lead leg. As an example, if your opponent is already preoccupied with trying to defend your lead leg roundhouse or side kicks, a well-timed hook kick can land cleanly on your opponent's head. The hook kick is usually thrown with the lead leg. A rear leg hook kick can be used, though like the rear leg side kick, has to travel a long way to its target, so be sure to set it up and to defend yourself before, during and after the technique.

To execute the lead leg hook kick, as with the side kick, raise your leg into a cocked-knee chamber whilst pointing the bottom of your heel at your opponent. From this position, shoot your leg out to about 10 inches to the side of your opponent's face. As your leg fully extends, retract your heel directly towards your opponent's face, landing the kick with the back of the heel. It is important to pivot on the ball of your supporting foot so that the back of its heel is pointed towards your opponent as your hook kick lands. Follow through with the kicking motion after the kick has landed before stepping your kicking foot down into your fighting stance.

1. Stance.

2. Lead hook kick chambered.

3. Extending leg.

4. Heel hooking back.

To advance when throwing the hook kick, push off the ball of your back foot and kick with your front foot at the same time. You can also slide-step to advance while throwing the lead leg hook kick (i.e. sliding the rear foot towards your lead foot before initiating the kick). Always throw your hook kick from a well-balanced position.

Keys to Success

- Chamber the knee and shoot a side kick about 10 inches to the side of your opponent's head, and pull your heel back across their face in a hooking motion.
- Twist your hips and shoulders, pointing your support foot in the opposite direction.
- Assume the proper body and foot position for the hook kick; don't let the toes point upward.
- Make contact with the heel.
- Keep your fists up by your face and your elbows in by your ribcage when throwing the kick.
- A well-executed hook kick is very difficult to defend against. Disguise your hook kick by making your opponent expect something else, then score with the hook kick to the head.

1. Rear axe kick swing.

The axe kick

The axe kick is unique in its trajectory and is difficult to defend against because of its angle of attack. The leg reaches perpendicular to the floor and drops straight down onto the head or clavicle of the opponent. Effective with either the lead or the rear leg, the axe kick is an effective technique that is used well by highly athletic and technical fighters, as a high level of flexibility is required to land an axe kick to the head.

2. Rear axe kick peak.

3. Rear axe kick drop.

From your fighting stance, bring your kicking leg to the inside of your centre line, keeping your leg as straight as possible *without* locking the knee. Continue lifting the leg in a narrow semi-circle until the leg is centred in front of your opponent. From there, thrust your hip forward as you use your gluteus and hamstring muscles to kick the leg straight down towards the opponent's head or clavicle. Extra reach and hip thrust can be accomplished by rotating the support foot in the opposite direction as you kick. To advance while throwing the axe kick, push forward off the ball of your support foot as you launch the kick at your target. Bring your leg back into your fighting stance as quickly as possible after throwing the kick. Keep your hands up and your chin down throughout the entire technique.

Keys to Success

- Bring your kicking leg high above your intended target before thrusting the kick down towards your opponent.
- Thrust your hips forward with the kick as you raise the heel of your supporting foot; push against the floor with the ball of your foot to obtain maximum leverage.
- Strike with the heel against the forehead, the face or the clavicle.
- Keep your fists up by your face, your chin tucked down, and your eyes on your opponent at all times during the execution of the kick.

Spinning kicks

Spinning kicks are extremely powerful techniques that can catch your opponent off guard, though there is a higher risk of counter-opportunity against you with spinning manoeuvres, as you need to turn before making contact with these kicks. Because of this, be sure to set up your spinning kicks effectively; it is good practice to throw a jab or similar set-up technique before throwing the kick. There are many kicks that are safer and more effective when thrown with a good set up, the prime examples being the spinning kicks illustrated in this chapter. When throwing a spinning kick, turn first, look over your shoulder and spot your target before shooting the leg out to score with the kick.

Spinning back kick

The spinning back kick carries tremendous power when thrown correctly. It is important to note that a correctly landed spinning back kick will usually cause you to turn back in the opposite direction, rather than continuing to spin around in a complete circle as with a spinning hook kick. If you were to continue to spin around in a complete circle after landing the kick, this is usually a sign that your force trajectory was not directly towards your opponent as it should have been, meaning your kick had less power than it should have. Focus on kicking *straight* towards your target, and this will put you in the proper position to turn back in the opposite direction, back into your stance. The most direct way to throw the spinning back kick from your stance is with the rear leg, as a lead leg spinning back kick will require you to step forward with your rear leg, or to momentarily 'switch' your stance, before you can throw the kick with the lead leg.

To throw a rear leg spinning back kick, start rotating your lead foot inward so your heel points towards your target, as you turn your shoulders and head in the same direction.

2. Rear spinning back kick chambered.

1. Rear spinning back kick pivot.

3. Rear spinning back kick extended.

Depending on how your stance is set up and the lateral distance between your feet (how close they are to the 'toe-to-heel line'), you may have to step across with your lead foot before beginning your rotation. As you continue turning, make sure to look over your rear shoulder as soon as possible to continue eye contact with the target. From this position, chamber your knee and instantaneously shoot your kick straight out towards your target. As with other kicks, avoid locking the leg out at the knee. Turn your body back in the opposite direction, back into your stance.

1. Rear spinning hook kick pivot.

Keys to Success

- Turn first! Initiate the spin and avoid throwing your kick prematurely.
- As you complete your turn to look over your opposite shoulder, make eye contact with your opponent immediately *before* you throw the kick.
- Chamber your kicking leg and shoot the kick straight out.
- Make contact with just the heel.

Spinning hook kick

The spinning hook kick travels in a circular motion, generating tremendous centrifugal force, and contact is made to the side of the head with the heel. As with the spinning back kick, the most direct way to throw the spinning hook kick is with the rear leg, as it does not require a step-through with the support leg to re-position the body during the technique. As with all spinning techniques, great attention has to be paid to the potential counter strikes available against you. The principle stands with every punch and kick: protect yourself before, during and after the technique.

2. Rear spinning hook kick swing.

To throw a rear leg spinning hook kick, begin by rotating your lead foot inward so

3. Heel hooking back.

your heel points towards your target, as you turn your shoulders and head in the same direction. Depending on how your stance is set up and the lateral distance between your feet (how close they are to the 'toe-to-heel line'), you may have to step across with your lead foot before beginning your rotation. As you continue to turn, make sure to look over your rear shoulder as soon as possible to continue eye contact with the target. This is the point during your body-rotation that you will fire your kick; your foot should travel parallel with your target for a distance of approximately 10 inches before contact is made. 'Hook' your kick through the target with the momentum of the spin. This will allow you to seamlessly return to your fighting stance as you 'follow through' with your kick in a circular motion.

Keys to Success

- Spin before you kick. Initiate the spin and avoid throwing your kick prematurely.
- Spot your target over your opposite shoulder before throwing the kick.
- Allow your kick to travel parallel with your target from a distance of about 10 inches before making contact.
- Strike with just the heel, allowing the hooking motion and circular rotation of the kick to pull you back into your stance.

Kicking strategy

It is important to utilize your kicks in a varied and deceptive manner. From long range, your kicks effectively set up follow-up techniques and combinations. Mix up your kicks to your opponent's body and head. For example, if your opponent has been hit by your lead leg side kick to their body, they're likely to focus their defence on protecting their mid-section. Even if they don't appear to be hurt, they will have felt the body attack. This is an opportunity to make your next kick a lead or rear leg roundhouse to the head – you've got their attention low; now hit them high. Likewise, if you score with a kick to the face, you can follow up with a hard rear leg roundhouse to the body.

Sweeps

Foot sweeps are a tactic to off-balance your opponent in order to set up techniques and combinations. Time your sweeps wisely to create offensive opportunities. All sweeps must be executed 'boot-to-boot'. Use a sweep and follow up with a punch while your opponent is off-balanced.

1. Stance.

2. Sweep.

3. Follow-up punch.

Keys to Success

- Make contact 'boot-to-boot' to off-balance your opponent.
- Follow up your sweep with a punch, kick or combination.
- Protect yourself with your hands up and chin down at all times.

FOOTWORK AND MOVEMENT

High-quality footwork is important in many sports such as soccer and tennis, but in no other sport is it more important than in Kickboxing. Skilful footwork can get a boxer out of dangerous situations and provide counter-punching opportunities. Developing smooth and balanced footwork is also essential for an effective Kickboxing workout. Footwork should be calculated and have a purpose. Use your legs

James uses footwork and movement to avoid opponents' attacks.

and feet to get you into and out of punching range. Stay relaxed and in control. Maintain your balance and stay on the balls of your feet. This will allow you to move smoothly across the floor.

Throughout the history of the sport, Kickboxers such as Don Wilson, Curtis Bush, Rick Roufus, and Massimo Brizi have taken imaginative footwork and ingenious movement in the ring to a balletic art form. Watch footage of how their balance, rhythm, and ability to change direction look almost effortless.

Forward movement

Smooth footwork and balanced movement allow you to get into range to land your punches. Starting from stance, push off the ball of your back foot as you move your front foot forward. Think in terms of 'pushing off' instead of 'stepping'. Both feet move almost simultaneously with your lead foot moving a split second first. If you take a large step with the front foot first, your weight will be placed on the heel instead of the ball of the front foot, making it difficult to change direction quickly. Pushing off keeps you on the balls of your feet and allows you to move quickly and pivot easily.

Backward movement

Kickboxers require quick, balanced movement to avoid an opponent's punches. Move backward by pushing off your front foot at the same time as the rear foot moves back. The purpose of this movement is to reset and plan your next move, either by throwing punches or moving once again in another direction.

Moving to your lead side

Effortless lateral movement is essential for boxers. Keep your feet shoulder-width apart in order to maintain your balance. To move to your lead side, push off your right foot as your left foot moves to the left. Stay in your Kickboxing stance with your upper body at a 45-degree angle, and not standing square to the target. This movement is not a lunge and should be kept compact.

Moving right to your rear side

When moving to the right, push off your lead foot as you move your rear foot to your rear side. Always stay in the correct Kickboxing stance when moving.

Keys to Success

- When moving forward, push off the ball of your back foot at the same time as you move your front foot forward.
- When moving backward, push off your front foot as your back foot moves backward.
- When moving to your lead side, push off your rear foot as your lead foot moves to your lead side.
- When moving to your rear side, push off your lead foot as you move your rear foot to your lead side.
- Do not try to cover ground too quickly by lunging or taking huge steps. This will put you off balance and in an awkward position.
- Do not cross your feet to change direction.
- Come back to the balanced on-guard position quickly, keeping your front foot and shoulder in the direction of the target.

Boxer's bounce

Boxer's bounce, also called boxing rhythm, refers to a style of movement that involves energetic bouncing and footwork similar to jumping rope. It is generally a forward and

Boxer's bounce.

backward movement that is balanced and subtle. The punches are timed with the bounce motion. This style of footwork keeps you light on your feet, provides cardio-conditioning, and burns more calories.

Watch fight footage of all-time great Kickboxers such as Don Wilson, Curtis Bush, Rick Roufus and Massimo Brizi. Notice how their rhythmic bouncing styles of constantly moving forward, backward, and side-to-side would confuse their opponents and create openings to land their own kicks and punches. Their foot movement was smooth and perfectly timed with the release of their punches.

Executing the Boxer's bounce

Start in your stance with your knees relaxed. Push off the balls of your feet, similar to jumping rope, and spring slightly forward, backward, and side-to-side. Stay on the balls of your feet while moving. Your heels do not touch the ground. To move forward, push off the ball of your rear foot and land on the ball of your lead foot. To move backward, push off the ball of your lead foot and land on the ball of your rear foot. This light and 'springy' motion is very subtle with your feet lifting just a few centimetres off the ground. You must briefly stop the bouncing motion in order to set your feet and throw your punches before returning to the bouncing rhythm. Bounce then set your feet, punch, and repeat.

Each foot pattern should be calculated to put you in position to strike your opponent or avoid counter-punches from your opponent. Practise this style of moving in 20- or 30-second spurts while shadowboxing or hitting the heavy bag. Focus on moving smoothly in all directions while staying balanced.

SHADOWBOXING

Shadowboxing is simply the raw exercise of moving your hands, feet, and body like a Kickboxer. Shadowboxing allows you to master the fluidity of a Kickboxer's movement. The punches, kicks, footwork, and defensive moves are combined to perform an effective workout without the need of a partner or a bag. Practising repetitive actions allows you to commit the Kickboxing movements to muscle memory. It is important to review the punching and kicking fundamentals and ensure your execution is accurate.

Shadowbox at the beginning of your training session. It is a great way to warm up the muscles of the body and also prepares you mentally for the workout to follow. When shadowboxing, always work on the correct execution of the punches and combine with foot movements. Often Kickboxers will fill up

1. Flicking jab.

2. Lead uppercut.

3. Cross.

their spare time between rounds of bag work and skipping with short bursts of shadowboxing, preparing themselves for the next session.

Your movements, kicks, punches, and foot patterns should follow a logical sequence and leave you in a balanced position, keeping in mind that all body and footwork movement needs to be free-flowing.

Constantly kick, punch and move, making use of whatever floor space is available. Shadowboxing is also a great time to practise new combinations and review basic fundamentals. Visualize an opponent in front of you and perform the necessary moves, be it attacking or defending. Shadowboxing puts you in the ring with your opponent.

Shadowboxing basics

Start by practising your footwork moving in a variety of directions, remembering to stay light on your feet and maintaining a balanced Kickboxing stance. Keep your hands in the on-guard position when you are shadowboxing.

Throw a few jabs as you move into position to strike your imaginary opponent and then move around. Review the technicalities of your jab ensuring the movement is smooth and accurate. Continue to move in multiple directions, throwing crisp jabs. As you become more comfortable with the single punches start to put two- and three-punch combinations together. Throw a jab, followed by a cross. This is the classic 'one-two' combination. Focus on throwing the combination smoothly and always return promptly to the on-guard position. This is a combination that you will return to over and over and is the starting point for many multiple punch combinations. Get creative and add variety to your combinations.

Shadowboxing.

Double up on your kicks. Do the same with your punches. Throw two fast roundhouse kicks, two jabs or two hooks consecutively. Visualize throwing punches to your opponent's body by bending your knees and lowering your body position. Throw a quick jab or a 'one-two' combination to the body. Now rise up quickly and throw some punches or a roundhouse kick in the direction of the head.

Focus on proper form. There is no benefit to throwing sloppy techniques. Ensure you are executing all moves correctly to develop positive muscle memory. Kicking and punching speed and power will come later.

2. Cross.

Punch sequencing

Boxing coaches often work with simple number sequences to designate specific punch combinations. The same punching methodology applies to Kickboxing. More detail will be given on number sequencing and kick-punch

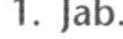

1. Jab.

3. Hook.

4. Uppercut.

combinations in Chapter 4. It is, however, a good idea to practise with the number sequencing while you are shadowboxing. The jab is the most important punch and is always designated as 'one'. The cross usually follows the jab and is designated as 'two'. The lead hook is identified as 'three' and the rear uppercut is known as 'four'.

As you execute a single punch, the movement should leave you in the correct position to deliver your next punch. If the first move puts you off balance slightly, the next move should bring you back on balance. An example of a combination that demonstrates the desired smooth transitional movements is a 'one-two-three' combination: a jab, followed by a cross and finishing with a lead hook. Start this combination by throwing a quick jab (one). Next your hips rotate as you pivot on your rear foot and a cross is launched (two). This should now leave you in position to throw a short, lead hook (three). As you deliver the lead hook, bring your hand back into the on-guard position, ready for your next punch. This simple three-punch combination teaches you to transfer your weight while pivoting on the balls of your feet and staying balanced. Practise this three-punch combination until you are proficient at it and then add on more punches.

Keep your combinations simple at first, as you decide what punches you want to throw and the desired location of your punch. If you are having trouble with your punch combinations, slow down your punches slightly, throw fewer punches and focus on proper form.

Keys to Success

- Bring your hands back to the on-guard position after every punch sequence.
- Use the floor space, never standing in one place.
- Maintain balance, timing your footwork with your punches.

DEFENSIVE MOVES

Mastering defensive moves is essential in order to become a successful Kickboxer. Incorporating slips, weaves, and feints adds an element of realism to your shadowboxing training. Both core and leg muscles are also required to perform defensive moves, making shadowboxing an effective workout.

Slips

One way in which Kickboxers avoid getting hit by punches is to 'slip' out of the way. Slipping utilizes a side-to-side motion of your head and upper body allowing evasion of an oncoming punch. Learning to slip effectively also allows Kickboxers to stay in range to throw counter-punches of their own.

Slip jab.

To slip punches, start with your hands up in the on-guard position and your body weight slightly forward, dip to the right or the left and immediately return to your original stance. Always keep your target in view. Although it is mostly an upper body move, the legs play an important role in slipping. Keep your knees bent and think of your legs as shock absorbers assisting in moving you quickly from side to side. Remain on the balls of your feet and do not lean back on your heels.

Incorporating slipping moves in between your punch combinations provides additional fitness benefits such as the use of your core muscles and the expenditure of more calories.

Slip a jab

Visualize a jab coming from your opponent and then dip to the outside of the punch, by shifting your body to the rear. Your rear knee bends slightly. Keep your hands up.

Slip cross.

Slip jab.

Slip a cross

Visualize a cross coming from your opponent and then dip to the outside of the punch, by shifting your body to your lead side. Your lead knee bends slightly. Keep your hands up.

Slip cross.

> **Keys to Success**
>
> - Make sure you do not over slip by shifting your weight too much to one side. Stay centred over your feet.
> - Keep your hands close to your chin in the on-guard protective position when slipping.

Bobbing and weaving

Another defensive move Kickboxers use to avoid getting hit is called 'bobbing and weaving' and it is used to avoid big powerful inside punches like hooks.

Starting in the on-guard position, start by turning away slightly from the direction of an incoming hook. Keep your back straight and bend both knees to 'drop' or lower your body in one quick motion. The motion is very similar to performing a quick squat. This is generally a small downward movement, not going any lower than 90 degrees at the knees. The idea is to duck just enough for the oncoming punch to safely go over the top of your head. After dropping to this position, 'weave' underneath the punch, allowing it to travel over your head

1. Bob and weave.

2. Bob and weave.

3. Bob and weave.

4. Bob and weave.

as your upper body travels in the opposite direction. Always return to your on-guard position as quickly as possible.

Incorporating bobbing and weaving into your punching routine will give you a more effective workout, challenging the core muscles, gluteus, hamstrings, and quadriceps.

Keys to Success

- Bend your knees to lower the body position. Bend at your waist only slightly.
- Stay on the balls of your feet as you duck. Do not lean backward.
- Keep ducking moves quick and concise.
- Do not bend too low.

Feints

A feint is a calculated action or movement with the intent to deceive your opponent. By making your opponent think you are going to do one thing then doing another, opportunities are created to land punches and kicks. You can use shoulder and arm feints to confuse your opponent. Pretend to punch, but do not throw the punch. You can chamber your leg as you

Feint jab.

skip forward but without throwing the kick. You can also use your feet to test your opponent's reaction by pretending to move in one direction, then moving in another direction. Pretend to direct a punch to one region of the body and then go to a different part of the body. For example, start by aiming your punch at the body region, but quickly redirect the punch to the head region. The same applies to your kicks. Start by throwing a lead leg roundhouse kick to the body, and as your opponent begins to react to it, quickly re-chamber the leg and fire the kick towards the face. Use feints strategically to test your opponent's defensive and counter-offensive habits and exploit them accordingly.

Executing basic feints

Shoulder feint

Jerk your lead shoulder forward as though you are going to throw a jab, but throw a straight right instead.

Foot feint

Half step with your front foot looking like you are moving to your lead side, then step back circling to your rear side and then throw a jab.

Punch feint
Swiftly move just your rear hand forward as if you are going to throw a cross and then come back with a lead hook.

Body punch feint
Bend your knees and drop down low in a position to throw a punch to the body region. Quickly rise up and throw a punch to the head region.

Roundhouse kick feint
Chamber your lead leg and start to extend a roundhouse kick to the body region. Quickly re-chamber the leg and throw the roundhouse to the face.

Side kick to punch feint
Chamber your lead leg and skip forward as if threatening to throw a side kick. Quickly place your lead foot back down without throwing the kick, and instead, fire off a hard cross or lead hook.

Remember you are trying to replicate a real fighting scenario. Adding feints to your punching routine while shadowboxing, working the focus pads and hitting the heavy bags makes for a more realistic shadowboxing experience. If you want to watch a master at feinting, view fight-footage of Bill 'Superfoot' Wallace.

Keys to Success

- Keep the movement subtle. Do not over exaggerate your feints.
- Practise in front of a large mirror to sharpen this skill and to ensure the movement is realistic.
- Return your fists to the on-guard position quickly so that you are in the correct position to execute your punches, and keep your fists up when kicking to protect yourself from any counter-attacks from your opponent.

Freestyle shadowboxing

Freestyle shadowboxing lets you practise all the punches, kicks and defensive moves. It allows you to get into the 'zone' and develop your own individual style. As you become proficient with basic combinations, start to improvise offensive and defensive moves, develop smooth transitions, and add slips, weaves, and feints. Your goal is to deliver fast-paced punches and kicks that flow easily and allow you to slip and counter-punch your opponent's techniques. Get in the zone by developing a Kickboxer's mentality. Would you give any less than 100 per cent if you were facing a live opponent? Visualize doing battle in the ring, focus and give your best effort. Enjoy the freedom of movement and the opportunity to create countless Kickboxing combinations that will be limited only by your own imagination.

Orthodox rear uppercut.

Southpaw rear uppercut.

EQUIPMENT

Gloves

There are essentially three types of gloves: boxing gloves, sparring gloves, and heavy bag gloves.

Boxing gloves

10oz boxing gloves are used in competitive matches and focus pad drills and are secured by either laces or Velcro straps. Many fighters use regular 10oz boxing gloves for working the bags as well.

Sparring gloves

16oz sparring gloves are used for sparring and training drills and can either have Velcro fasteners or laces. The extra padding weight of the gloves provides added protection for your hands and a larger surface area of impact surface on the glove. This reduces the risk of cuts to your sparring partner, along with the protection that headgear provides.

Heavy bag gloves

These gloves are smaller than regulation 10oz boxing gloves and are designed for working the heavy bag. While many fighters use boxing gloves to work the heavy bag, utilizing heavy bag gloves from time to time will reinforce good habits such as proper fist and wrist alignment, as they don't form your fist for you in the same way as boxing gloves do. Ensure there is adequate space inside the gloves, allowing for sufficient blood circulation. The gloves need to be snug around your hands and feel secure. They are generally made out of leather or synthetic materials.

Some fighters like to use one pair of gloves for all their training purposes. If this is what you prefer, you'll need bigger gloves for one reason: sparring. When you're sparring, you will need to wear at least 14–16oz gloves. So, if you prefer 10oz boxing gloves or heavy bag gloves for hitting bags and pads, then you will need to have at least two pairs of gloves.

Gloves.

Kick boots

Most quality kick boots that you'll find will be of the design standards for Full Contact Kickboxing training and competition. Slip your foot into

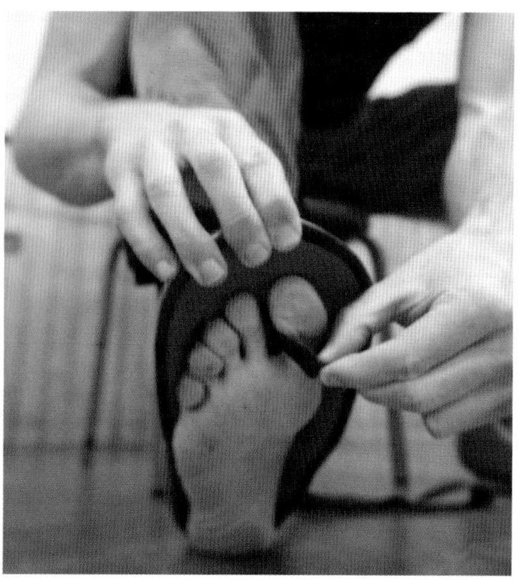

1. Kick boot.

2. Kick boot.

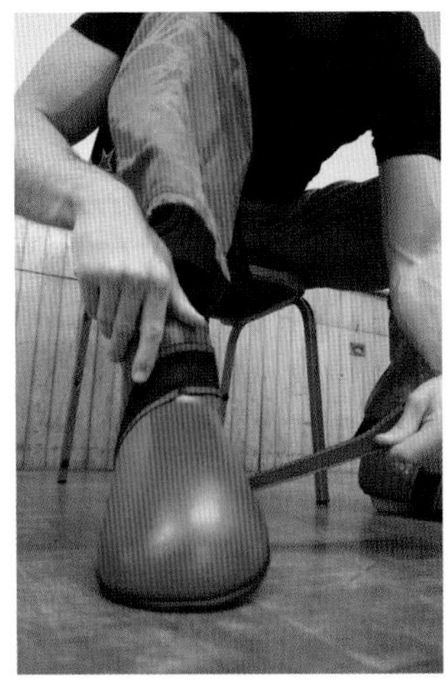
3. Kick boot.

4. Kick boot.

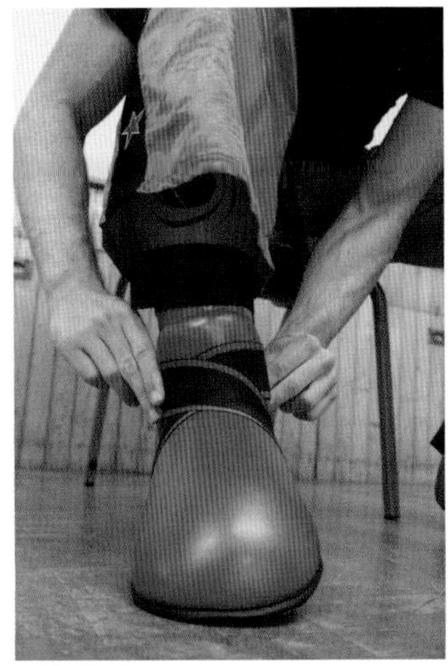
5. Kick boot.

the boot and secure your big toe in the loop underneath the front of the boot. Most boots have a fastening strap with a Velcro attachment that secures at the back of the heel. Loop the strap around your boot in an 'X' pattern and secure the Velcro at the back of the boot.

Shin guards

Your shin guards will often come in a set with your kick boots. If you don't have shin guards that match your boots, ensure that you find some that are designed for Full Contact Kickboxing. Fasten your shin guards with the Velcro straps around the calves. Ensure they're tight enough that they won't move around while you're training or fighting, but not so tight that they limit your ability to flex your calves and to move your feet at the ankle joints properly.

Shin guards.

3 WORKING THE BAGS

HEAVY BAG

The heavy bag is a tried-and-tested training tool that has shaped many champions in the ring. With an endless number of punching and kicking combinations available, it provides an exceptional workout that challenges your aerobic, anaerobic, and musculature systems.

Hook kick.

OPPOSITE: Working the bags.

Striking the larger bags provides an immense release of tension and improves muscular strength and endurance. Hitting the smaller bags develops speed and hand eye coordination, as well as testing and developing your agility and reaction time.

When training on the heavy bag, you must move and throw punches and kicks as though you have a real live opponent in front of you. The time you have put into your shadowboxing and mirror training, as well as practising the fundamentals, will benefit your transition to the heavy bag. Warm up properly and prepare to go into battle with your virtual opponent, the heavy bag.

Heavy bag basics

Proper stance

Start by establishing your stance in front of the bag. Fully extend your lead arm to make contact with the knuckle portion of your glove on the bag. Keep the wrist straight. Take a step back, moving 15cm (6in) away from the bag. This is the starting distance for working the bag and throwing punches. The moment your fist makes contact with the heavy bag, tighten your fist. Keep the hands in a semi-relaxed fist as you move around the bag. You will waste energy if you constantly hold your fist tight and stay too tense.

Range

Be aware of your distance from the heavy bag and stay slightly more than arm's length away. Your jab is your range finder, and it will give you a sense of how close you have to be to land other punches and kicks. Your straight punches will set up the short punches, such as hooks and uppercuts. Move your feet to get into range to strike the bag.

Create space

Determine your maximum punching distance. Throw some jabs ensuring your arm is fully extended as your glove makes contact with the centre of the bag. Make sure you are not standing too close to the bag – keep a realistic distance from your virtual or imaginary opponent. The aim is to maintain a consistent distance between you and the heavy bag.

Proper punching technique

Focus on throwing crisp punches aiming to hit the centre of the bag. When throwing jabs and crosses, your arms should be almost fully extended upon impact. As soon as your glove

1. Jab.

2. Cross.

3. Lead hook.

4. Rear hook.

5. Lead uppercut to body.

6. Rear uppercut to body.

7. Jab to body.

makes impact with the bag, quickly return your fists to the on-guard position ready to throw your next punch. Your punch should jolt the bag with a quick, snapping motion. If you leave the punch out there too long, you are pushing the bag, resulting in a sloppy, lazy punch. Keep your neck, shoulders, and arms relaxed and this will assist in throwing fast, snapping punches. 'Lead with speed; follow with power.' Never sacrifice technique for punching power. Start by throwing light, quick punches, gradually adding more power and use your imagination as you build two- and three-punch combinations.

'Punch and get out'

As you continue to establish your range and move around the bag, step forward with your punches and then step back. This is called 'punch and get out'. At the moment of impact, keep your core muscles tight and return your hands to the on-guard position quickly. Pivot on the balls of your feet when throwing punches to maintain balance. This provides a stable stance from which maximum power can be executed. Never stand flat-footed: always stay on the balls of your feet ready to move in any direction. Once you have found your range with your jab, try throwing some crosses, and one-two combinations.

Natural swinging motion

Incorporate the slight swinging motion of the bag into your punching rhythm as the heavy bag will swing in a natural motion when it is hit properly. You want to use this motion to time your punches while you move around the bag. A technically correct crisp punch will jolt the bag but not make it move excessively. Coordinate your footwork with the swinging motion of the bag and time your strikes by ensuring that your punches make solid contact with the bag as it comes towards you. Pushing your punches and not snapping them will create unnecessary swinging of the bag. Throwing wild punches or whaling at the bag as it is moving away will also cause the bag to swing uncontrollably, and you will never develop a good rhythm.

Keep moving

'Float like a butterfly, sting like a bee.'

Find a consistent punching pace that you can continue with and persevere to the end of the round. Keep up a steady punching pace for the entire 2 minutes of every round and use your 1-minute rest to recover between rounds. When performing this type of interval training, you may have the tendency to hit the bag vigorously for the first 30 to 40 seconds and then be too winded to continue punching for the remainder of the round. Remember to pace yourself.

Breathe naturally

Mix it up.

The body tenses up while punching the heavy bag and there is often a tendency to hold your breath for a split second. Stay relaxed and exhale as you throw your punches, then breathe in to get a new supply of oxygen to your working muscles. To perform any type of aerobic activity, proper exhalation is important. Find a natural breathing rhythm that suits you. Exhale on exertion and then inhale to replenish the oxygen to the body.

Keys to Success

- Focus on proper execution and punching technique.
- Establish a realistic distance from the bag, slightly more than a jab's distance away. Your arm should be almost fully extended on impact when throwing straight punches.
- Nothing stays still in the ring. Make sure you move around while throwing punches.
- Snap your punches to avoid excessive swing of the heavy bag. Time your punches to make contact with the bag as it moves slightly towards you.
- Do not drop your hands after punching. This will leave you out of position for your next series of punches.

Defensive moves

Add slipping and bobbing and weaving moves into your heavy bag punching combinations to challenge your core and leg muscles. These defensive moves add another level of realism and intensity to your heavy bag workout, and they help prepare you for pad work and sparring.

Slipping

The slipping movement engages the core muscles of the torso. With your hands in the protective position, imagine your opponent

Slipping.

throwing a jab. Slip the punch by dipping to the outside of it, making sure your eyes are always on your opponent. After slipping, you can counter with a rear punch to the body. Slip a cross by bending your knees and lowering your body outside of the punch. Counter by throwing a lead hook.

Slipping 'outside' of a punch means that you move your head to the side of your opponent's straight punch where your head is then 'in the clear' from your opponent's other hand. If you slip 'inside' a punch, you move your head directly in line with your opponent's other hand, making you potentially more vulnerable to their follow-up punch.

Although you may occasionally see Kickboxing Champions slip 'inside' a punch to look for a counter opportunity, this is a reflection of highly tuned skills and reactions; it should only be done if you're a professional or very advanced in your training. In general, it is safer for beginning to intermediate practitioners to slip to the outside of a punch, where there will be many counter opportunities available to you.

Bobbing and weaving

Bobbing and weaving.

Bobbing and weaving is another defensive move that provides fitness benefits. It involves engagement of the gluteals, quadriceps and core muscles. By using your legs to lower your body and move under a punch (bobbing), the body shifts from one side to the other (weaving). When you weave under a punch to the left, counter back with a left hook, and when you weave under and over to the right, counter with a right hook.

Blocking

Practising blocking when you're working on the heavy bag helps create actual combat scenarios. Keeping your hands up high in the on-guard position, your core muscles tight, and your gloves against your head, imagine your opponent throwing a jab, cross or a hook and imagine blocking the punch. Simulate defending a lead hook by blocking the punch with your rear glove and turning your body slightly with the direction of your opponent's hook. This is called 'rolling' with the punch. From here, you can throw a lead hook counter-punch to the bag. Blocking a

Blocking.

cross from your opponent with your lead glove will put you in prime position to counter with a rear uppercut to the body; particularly when you roll with the punch as you block it. Remember to keep your eyes on your target throughout all of these defensive movements.

Visualization

Visualizing an opponent keeps the workout interesting and will motivate you to work harder.

Visualization.

Heavy bag punch combinations

Basic combinations

Double and triple jabs

Throw two or three rapid-fire jabs. Focus on speed not power when throwing double and triple jabs. Execute a stronger first jab and follow with the second or third jab by flicking fast and light with no pause between the jabs. The second and third jabs are executed by pulling back approximately one-third the distance of the first jab. It is all about speed, moving your opponent off-balance, and setting up to throw more powerful punches.

Heavy bag combinations.

Jab to the body – jab to the head

Lower your body position and step forward as you launch a quick jab to the body (dead centre just below the mid-portion of the bag). Now raise your body position and immediately launch a jab to the head region. After you land your second jab, quickly step away from the bag ready to throw your next combination.

The one-two

Throw a fast jab followed immediately by a powerful cross, returning both hands quickly to the on-guard position. Move away from the bag ready to throw your next combination. Throw one-twos to the head and one-twos to the body. To throw a one-two combination to the body, bend your legs to lower your position and aim your punches to the mid-section of the bag. Ensure your hands are in the correct on-guard position. This classic punch sequence is utilized more than any other combination.

One-two – lead hook

Move forward as you launch a quick one-two combination (jab, cross). You should now be in position to throw a short, lead hook to complete the combination. Move away from the bag and get ready to throw your next punch sequence.

Basic five-punch combo: double jab to the body – single jab to the head – cross – lead hook

Lower your body throwing two quick, light jabs to the mid-section of the bag. Move up and throw a hard jab to the head, followed by a cross to the head. Pivot and throw a short, lead hook to the head.

Slip combo: jab to the head – slip – cross – lead hook to the body

Lead with a jab to the head. Visualize a jab coming from your opponent and slip outside of the punch. Immediately come back with a cross to the head and dig in with a lead hook to the body. Make sure your hands are up when you slip, remembering to pivot on the balls of your feet; shift your weight to add power to your punches.

Jab – rear uppercut – lead hook – short cross

Fire a jab to the head, move forward and throw a rear uppercut to the body, followed by a lead hook to the head and then finish with a short rear hand to the head.

Intermediate/advanced combinations

One-two – double lead hook

Lower your body position and throw a quick one-two to the mid-section. Follow up with a fast lead hook to the body and immediately rise up and throw your second lead hook to the head. Both hooks need to be in quick succession without a pause.

Feint jab – cross – lead hook – cross

With your lead fist, appear to throw the jab, hold back, and then launch your rear hand to the head instead. Next throw a lead hook to the head and finish with another cross to the head. As mentioned earlier, feints are designed to fool your opponent. Feints make it appear that you are going to throw one punch, but you throw a different punch. They need to be quick, subtle, and realistic. Incorporate feints into your other punch combinations.

Punch flurries

Flurries are light, crisp, fast, punches thrown in bunches. Throw four to six rapid-fire punches at a time. The delivery is fast so there is no time to load up on your punches. Just let your hands go.

Heavy bag punch kick combinations

Roundhouse kick.

When you have developed a groove with the basic and intermediate/advanced punch combinations on the heavy bag, this is a good time to begin adding kicks to your heavy bag workout. Keep the same attention to technical precision and quality work when training punch-kick combinations as when training only your punches. Keep your jab sharp, move with control and balance, and execute your kicks with the same quality as your hand techniques. As always, keep your chin down and your hands up during and between all of the following combinations.

Jab – cross – rear leg roundhouse kick
This great basic combination can be thrown with speed and power to develop fluidity in combinations. It can also be used frequently and to great effect in Kickboxing matches. Throw a quick and sharp one-two (jab, cross) combination and immediately follow up with a roundhouse kick. Right after your cross lands, continue the momentum by throwing your kick with no hesitation. This is a great combination for setting up the roundhouse kick to the head, but as you practise this combo, 'mix it up' between throwing your roundhouse kick to the head and to the body. Speed, accuracy

1. Jab.

2. Cross.

3. Rear roundhouse.

and good technique make this combination hard to beat.

Jab – cross – lead leg roundhouse kick
Throw a fast jab followed immediately by a powerful cross. As you bring your rear hand back to your face, begin to slide your rear foot to your lead foot before launching a powerful roundhouse kick with your lead leg, making contact

1. Jab.

2. Cross.

3. Lead roundhouse.

with the instep or the lower shin, depending on your distance from the bag. Rotate your hips and shoulders forcefully to generate power with this kick. Step back into your stance after the combination, moving away from the bag to establish your range and ready yourself for another combination. As before, vary between throwing the kick to the body and the head as you practise this combination, while keeping the punches to the head with each repetition.

Jab – lead body hook – rear leg roundhouse kick to the head

Launch your jab to the face and then dip down to rip a hard body hook off with the lead hand.

1. Jab.

2. Lead body hook.

3. Rear roundhouse.

Immediately follow with a rear roundhouse up-high.

Rear body hook – lead head hook – rear leg roundhouse kick

Just as a cross is sometimes thrown first, so can a rear hook to the body: a particularly potent and damaging punch that is often hard for opponents to anticipate and defend against in Kickboxing – especially if you set it up effectively. This combination is a great counter-combination immediately after you have blocked your opponent's techniques on your guard. 'Rip the body' with a hard rear body hook followed immediately by the lead head hook and the rear roundhouse kick. While this is a great combination with which to use

1. Rear body hook.

2. Lead hook.

3. Rear roundhouse.

the roundhouse kick to the head, vary between throwing the kick to the head and to the body.

Lead leg front kick – one-two – lead hook – rear leg roundhouse kick

From long range, move forward with a quick lead leg front kick to the body. After the kick lands, step down into your stance as you launch a quick one-two combination (jab, cross). You should now be in position to throw a short, lead hook. After your hook lands, rotate your body in the opposite direction and launch a powerful rear leg roundhouse kick. Depending on the range between you and the heavy bag, you may need to step in the direction of your kick before launching it, in order to avoid jamming your own technique. Vary

2. Jab.

1. Lead front kick.

3. Cross.

4. Lead hook.

Rear front kick.

5. Rear roundhouse.

between throwing the kick to the body and the head as you practise this combination, while keeping the punches to the head and the front kick to the body with each repetition.

Lead leg front kick – one-two – lead hook – rear leg front kick – jab

From long range, move forward with a quick lead leg front kick to the body. After the kick lands, step down into your stance as you launch a quick one-two combination (jab, cross). You should now be in position to throw a short, lead hook. After your hook lands, chamber your rear leg and shoot out a front kick to the body. Finish the combination with a jab to re-establish your range; as soon as the front kick goes to the body and the opponent's defence is lowered, you snap a jab to the face.

Lead leg side kick – one-two – lead head hook – high rear leg roundhouse kick

Lead side kick.

Lead by moving in with a side kick to the body. Re-chamber your kicking leg and step it down into your stance – immediately following up with a one-two (jab, cross). Depending on how much you've caused the heavy bag to swing with your side kick, you may need to advance with your jab. After landing your one-two punch combo, immediately follow with a lead hook to the head and a rear roundhouse kick; varying between the head and the body as you practise this combination. Return to your stance and move out of range after landing the full combination.

Jab – cross – lead hook – lead leg hook kick
Shoot your jab out and follow with a cross and lead hook to the head. After your hook punch lands, immediately follow up with a lead leg hook kick. All techniques in this combination are aimed at head-height.

Lead hook kick.

Rear body hook – lead body hook – rear uppercut – lead hook – high rear roundhouse kick
From close range, dip your weight onto your back leg as you bob your head in the same direction. From there, drop your rear hand halfway down and throw a hard hook to the body. Immediately follow up with a lead hook to the body, a rear uppercut to the chin and a lead hook to the head, shifting your body-weight with each punch. After the hook lands, launch a powerful rear leg roundhouse kick to the head. Depending on the range between you and the heavy bag, you may need to step in the direction of your kick before launching it, in order to avoid jamming your own technique.

Rear uppercut.

One-two – lead leg roundhouse kick to the body – cross-hook – rear leg roundhouse kick to the head
A great combination to train your 'machine-gun' punch-kick-punch-kick ability, as well as being a highly effective combination in the ring. Step in with your one-two and quickly step your rear foot towards your lead leg to facilitate a hard lead roundhouse to the body. Step down into your stance and immediately fire off a cross, lead hook and rear roundhouse kick, each shot aimed to the head. In combat, this is a great combination with which to build forward momentum, but be aware of your range when drilling it on the heavy bag. The bag won't move back like an opponent would when under assault from these rapid punches and kicks.

Building combinations

Building combinations.

Imagine you are facing an elusive opponent who is constantly moving while throwing techniques at you. When facing this type of opponent, you must move continuously. You will either move while throwing your combinations, or 'plant your feet' to throw a series of techniques, and then immediately start moving around the bag again. 'Planting your feet' means momentarily staying in one position to throw a combination; it does *not* mean standing flat-footed. Always keep your weight in the balls of your feet. Even when planting your feet to throw combinations, you must still pivot on the balls of your feet with every punch and kick. Keep moving and throw plenty of jabs to set up your power punches.

Sample workout

This sample workout includes ten rounds. Make sure to rest for 1 minute after each round of work. For more extensive and detailed workouts, refer to Chapter 10.

Shadowbox: 3 × 2-minute rounds

The first round is a warm-up round. Focus on proper techniques, going through your basic punches and kicks. Keep your feet moving and focus on your foot work. Your heart rate will increase.

For rounds two and three, put more combinations together and increase your work rate. Throw your punches and kicks with focus and real fighting intent. Continue to practise high quality footwork and movement.

Skip: 3 × 2-minute rounds

Jump at a challenging pace, and mix up the foot work. Perform three rounds.

Heavy bag: 3 × 2-minute rounds

Start with the basic punches and kicks; add more combinations and power with each round. Perform three rounds.

Shadowbox: 1 × 2-minute round

This is a cool-down round and will lower your heart rate. Punch with little intent. Perform one round.

Keys to Success

- Move around and incorporate the natural swinging motion of the bag into your workout.
- Work the bag like you are facing a real opponent.
- Start with the basic techniques and slowly build multiple kick-punch combinations.
- Add slipping and bobbing and weaving movements while working the bag.
- Stay on the balls of your feet. Never stand flat-footed.

Choosing a heavy bag

Whether you are training at home, at a fitness club, or working out at a Boxing or Kickboxing gym, there are numerous styles and sizes of heavy bags specific to your training requirements.

Choosing a bag depends on a few variables. If you are new to hitting the heavy bag you want a softer bag: 30kg (60lb) to 36kg (80lb). If the bag is too dense, the punching impact over time can stress the muscles and joints of the hands, arms and shoulders. If you are experienced, you will want to strike a more solid bag: 36kg (80lb) to 55kg (120lb).

Another consideration is your actual weight. It is often suggested that you should use a bag that is approximately half your body weight.

Body weight	Heavy bag
63kg (139lb or less)	27kg (60lb)
64–72kg (140–159lb)	36kg (80lb)
73–82kg (160–180lb or more)	45+kg (100+lb)

Reactive bags

The smaller bags, such as the speed bag and double-end bag, require more technical skills, quick responsive movement, and finesse. More patience is required, but the payoff is worth it.

Reactive bags.

SPEED BAG

A speed bag is a small punching bag suspended below a platform (horizontal backboard) on a swivel hook, allowing for free rotational movement. It can be mounted on the wall or from a stand. The exterior is made of leather and this is filled with an air bladder. A variety of sizes are available with the smaller

Speed bag training.

bags approximately 10cm (8in) in length. They move fast, and rebound quickly, making them a greater challenge to hit. The largest speed bags are around 20cm (14in) long. These react more slowly and are easier to hit than the smaller bags.

The 'speed' bag is the perfect name for this timeless piece of training equipment. The bag rebounds off the backboard as fast as you hit it, forcing you to keep pace and an accurate rhythm.

Speed bag benefits

Speed bag training develops the upper body and shoulder musculature, and perfects hand–eye coordination. This training works on your timing, speed, and accuracy. It also places a demand on your cardiovascular system and improves your endurance.

The speed bag develops lightning-fast reaction time which can easily translate to all sports. In any sport you are active in, such as hockey, baseball, soccer, rugby, football, volleyball, and racquet sports (tennis and squash), speed bag training will improve your overall performance.

Speed bag benefits.

Adjusting the speed bag

Adjusting the speed bag.

The bottom of the speed bag should be at eye level if you are using a small speed bag. For a larger speed bag, the bag should be 1–2 inches above your chin. Some speed bag platforms are adjustable so the bag can be moved to the appropriate level for you.

The bag needs to be firm, but not rock hard. If you are having difficulty hitting the bag, let some of the air out of the bladder and it will slow down the bag movement, allowing you more control.

1. First strike.

2. Bag rebounds.

3. Be ready to strike again.

Heavy bag basics

Hitting the speed bag: triplet rhythm

The rhythm of hitting the speed bag is called a 'triplet' rhythm as the bag rebounds three times, forward-backward-forward, with each strike. So the sequence is 'strike-1-2-3'. With the first strike, the bag moves away and hits the back portion of the platform (1). It then rebounds and hits the front portion of the platform (2). The bag rebounds away once again to hit the back portion of the platform (3). This is the precise moment you strike the bag once again.

Proper form

Step 1

Stand facing square to the bag with both shoulders at an equal distance from the bag. You do not have to be in the boxer's stance. Bring both fists up in front of your face, your arms bent (with the elbows bent at about 90 degrees) and tucked in by the sides of your body. Your fists are approximately 15–20cm (6–8in) away from the bag.

Step 2

Strike the bag in the centre making sure your knuckles land flush against the leather. Hit straight through the bag. Ensure you are not 'chopping' at the bag with your strikes. Instead visualize hitting through the bag. Once you strike the bag, immediately circle your fist back to the starting position.

Step 3

Repeat striking the bag with the 'strike-1-2-3' rhythm remembering to keep both hands up by your face. It is often the transition from striking with one hand to the other that breaks your rhythm and causes ineffective hits. Start with six to eight strikes with one hand until

Proper form.

you become competent. Switch to the other hand. Everyone has a dominant hand, so stick with it until both hands are performing equally. Reduce the number of repetitions to four hits, down to two, and then singles.

Step 4

Single strikes. As you make contact with the bag with one hand, the opposite hand immediately comes up ready to strike the bag. Repeat, keeping this semi-circular movement concise and fast. As your punch speed increases, the circular range of motion your arm goes through will become shorter. The single strike is more challenging, as the faster pace requires you to react sooner.

Focus your strikes

The area where your knuckles make contact on the bag and how hard you strike it will affect your ability to keep the bag under control. If you make contact with the bag too soon,

Focus your strikes.

a clumsy and awkward rhythm will result. If you strike the bag too late, your fist will hit the underside of the bag. When starting out use medium force until you have mastered the punching rhythm.

Listen to the rhythm

As you make faster contact with the bag it is more difficult to see the rebounds, but you will still be able to hear the sounds. The triplet sequence has a distinct sound and paying attention to these sounds will assist you in developing a smooth punching rhythm. The first sound is the bag hitting the back of the platform after you strike it. The second sound is the bag moving forward and hitting the front of the platform. The third sound is the rebound of the bag moving away from you and hitting the back of the platform once again.

As you become more proficient, increase your punch speed. Wearing hand wraps provides sufficient protection for your knuckles when striking the speed bag; however, if you want more protection for your hands, use speed bag striking mitts or glove wraps. The mitts have a flat punching surface and are lightly padded for extra protection. The design of the glove wraps is a combination of mesh, neoprene, and a shock-absorbing gel over the knuckle region, providing extra comfort and protection.

Open-hand method

If you have difficulty controlling the speed bag, use the open-hand striking method to improve your technique. Address the bag straight-on so both hands have an equal reach to the speed bag. Keep your hands open, your palms facing the bag and drive the centre of the bag forward with your open hand. Spreading the fingers wide apart allows for more contact time with the bag and better control. Allow the bag to roll off your fingers in a straight swinging motion. Follow through, bringing your hands straight back. This open-handed method will help slow down the pace of the movement of the bag for beginners until you become more efficient with the 'strike-1-2-3' rhythm. Follow the steps below, with open hands.

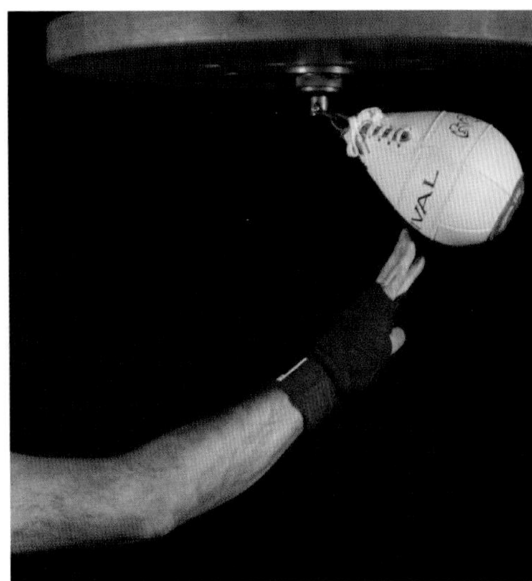

Open hand method.

Speed bag punch combinations

Four strikes

Four strikes with each hand allow you to get a rhythm established before you switch to the other hand. A great way to start!

Double strikes

Reducing down to double strikes means you are bringing your other hand into play sooner.

Single strikes

Strike alternating hands. The transition from your right fist to your left fist is quick and needs to be smooth.

Strikes with movement

Alternate strikes with each hand, while circling the platform. Try to keep the bag steady as you are moving.

Keys to Success

- Assume the standard speed bag stance, with your feet about shoulder width apart. Have your body facing the bag straight on to ensure that both arms have equal reach.
- Strike the bag, moving your arms in small circles.
- Bring your fists back up to striking level after hitting the bag. (Keeping your hands low will throw your timing off.)
- Hit the bag lightly to maintain control.
- Make contact with the belly of the speed bag: not too high, nor too low.

Free-style

Effortlessly go from multiple strikes to single strikes, varying your speed and rhythm. This can include short bursts of rapid-fire punching for 15 to 20 seconds and then back to a regular pace. Mix it up.

Use a smaller speed bag to challenge and improve your agility and hand–eye coordination. Vary the speed of the punches, slower punches interspersed with sprints. Once you have your rhythm down, move around the bag while punching.

THE DOUBLE-END PUNCHING BAG

The random rebounding action of the double-end striking bag simulates the movement of an actual opponent. This improves reaction time and forces you to quickly make small adjustments on your punch execution and defensive moves.

Sometimes referred to as a floor-to-ceiling ball, double-end bags are round, lightweight, inflatable sacks made of leather that are suspended

Double end bag.

Focus.

vertically by a bungee or shock cord from the ceiling and anchored to the floor. They come in various sizes with the smaller bags being the most challenging to hit. How quickly the bag rebounds and how far it swings are also influenced by the tension of the shock cords.

Working on the double-end bag improves the speed and accuracy of your punch combinations. It also gives you an opportunity to work on defensive techniques such as slipping movements. The intention behind this reactive

Ready to follow up.

Slip right.

Slip left.

piece of equipment is to challenge your coordination, timing, and agility. Save your heavy hitting power for the heavy bag.

The muscles of the shoulders, upper back, and core are recruited in order to strike the bag and must respond quickly.

It is best to wear gloves when hitting the double-end bag. Gloves give you more control because of the larger contact surface and they also protect your hands. When you strike the double-end bag it will move quickly away, then rebound back at you. Keep your hands in the on-guard position and your gloves held firmly in front of your head. This will prevent the bag from making contact with your face. Either counter with a punch or slip out of the way.

2. Aim for the centre of the bag.

Starting out

Get in your fighting stance: hands up, and more than a jab's length away from the bag. Ensure you are far enough away from the bag so the bag will not rebound and hit you. It is from this

1. Study how the bag rebounds.

3. Slipping.

position that you want to execute some jabs. Study how the bag rebounds back at you, at what angle, and the speed it travels. It may seem as though the bag has a mind of its own.

Aim for the centre of the bag. If the bag is spiralling off to one side, you are not catching it dead centre. The movement of the bag should be forward and backward without any side-to-side motion when you strike it. Initially develop a sense of timing and discover how the bag reacts to your single straight punches (a jab and a cross), before moving on to combinations.

Keys to Success

- Keep your fists up by your chin, elbows close to your body and eyes on the target.
- Focus on striking the bag flush and dead centre.
- Throwing hard, wild punches on the double-end bag will cause it to move erratically. Instead, strike the bag with light, crisp, punches. This will enable you to develop a smooth punch rhythm.
- Save the power and strength for the heavy bag.
- When slipping, practise moving your head and shoulders just enough to avoid the rebound of the bag. If the slips are over-exaggerated, it will throw you off-balance and put you out of position to counter-punch effectively.
- Maintain a balanced stance, staying on the balls of your feet.

The unique qualities of the various large bags and the reactive bags challenge your fitness capabilities, your mental focus, and develop your skill levels and your physicality. Always execute your techniques and movements utilizing proper technique. If you make this commitment to challenge yourself, improvements in timing, hand–eye coordination, quick reflexes, agility, speed, and power will be achieved. Improvements in your cardiovascular fitness, upper and lower body muscular strength, definition, and endurance, core strength, and balance will all be enhanced.

The quick reflexes and fast movements that result from training on the large bags and reactive bags provide a dynamic training experience unlike any other workout.

A dynamic training experience.

4 WORKING THE FOCUS PADS

Focus pad training can be an incredibly dynamic and challenging training tool. Because working with a skilled pad holder is the closest thing to replicating a sparring session, focus pad training is an incredibly effective method of improving technical skills, as well as developing precise synchronization of speed, power, and accuracy.

Focus pads are hand-held padded mitts made from dense foam covered by leather or vinyl. The pads are held by a training partner or by a coach. The catcher (coach) and the striker (Kickboxer) work together to create an effective training scenario. The catcher gives clear and concise directions to the striker, who in turn responds quickly and skilfully. If an experienced coach is not available, choose a training partner with a similar skill level. Working together as a team is the key when training on focus pads and learning both roles is essential.

Focus pad training is a blank canvas allowing you to create an engaging and responsive workout experience. You get to work on offence and defence simultaneously. It requires complete mental focus and coordination.

Focus pad work requires focus and coordination.

Hold pads in correct position.

OPPOSITE: Focus pad training.

There are many unique advantages of focus pad training: you receive instantaneous feedback from the catcher, and since you are continuously moving around a live partner, your reactive skills are challenged, and improvements are assured.

Working together.

FOCUS PAD FUNDAMENTALS

The catcher

The catcher must clearly and concisely call out combinations and be ready to receive the punches and kicks. The catcher sets the pace by giving instructions to their partner and must be comfortable controlling the action. Basic number sequences can be assigned for specific punches and combinations.

The catcher calls out a number or a technique and the striker throws the appropriate punch or kick. Controlling what move is coming allows the catcher to angle the pad properly and anticipate the force of the technique. The catcher counterbalances the force by 'feeding' the pad into each blow.

Catcher basics

When working pads with a partner, your arm position is similar to the on-guard stance, with the palms turned towards your partner ready to receive a strike. Keep your elbows slightly bent to absorb the impact of the incoming punches and kicks. Maintain stability in the body, legs, and feet by staying in the classic Kickboxer's stance. Always keep your eyes on your partner and clearly communicate the combinations to be executed.

The catcher's job is to have the pads in the correct position to receive the punches and kicks. When catching straight punches, the pads need to be facing forward. When catching hooks, turn the palm of the pad inward. When catching uppercuts, turn the palm of the pad downward, towards the floor. To receive straight kicks such as front kicks and side kicks, angle the pads forward. To receive circular kicks such as roundhouse and hook kicks, turn the pads inward. Depending on the force of

Don't tune out

Stay focused on your technique and on your partner so you can time and angle the pads to safely catch the techniques. It's important not to let your mind wander. Be mindful and encourage and challenge your partner.

Work together

The catcher selects the combinations and sets the pace of each round. It is crucial for the striker to pay attention to all instructions from the catcher. Both must focus on the task, working together to create a safe training environment and developing smooth transitions between combinations. Work hard and always give your best effort.

a given kick, you may choose to place one pad on top of the other, or brace both pads together, side-by-side, to absorb the impact of the kick.

For head-height techniques, the pads are generally held around shoulder level, but will need to be lowered slightly if training with a shorter partner or raised slightly if training with a taller partner. When two orthodox partners are working with the pads, the left focus pad catches the jab and the right focus pad catches the cross. The same follows for hooks and uppercuts.

The catcher provides dynamic resistance by moving the pads forward slightly to meet the incoming techniques. This is called 'feeding' the punches and kicks. This provides the proper feel, distance, and resistance for the striker. The receiving and resisting motion helps to reduce the impact on the catcher's shoulders. Catching kicks and punches can be a workout in itself, so be prepared by warming up the arms and shoulders beforehand.

Tips for catching for a 'southpaw'

When an orthodox catcher is working with a 'southpaw' Kickboxer, the catcher always mimics the 'southpaw' stance with the right foot forward. The catcher stands with the right foot forward, catches the 'southpaw' right jab with the right pad and catches the left cross with the left pad. The right pad catches the right hooks and uppercuts, and the left pad catches the left hook and uppercuts.

The striker

Working on focus pad drills with a partner allows you to perfect your techniques while moving and responding quickly to changing circumstances. The catcher mimics the movement of an actual opponent. Unlike working on the heavy bag, the target continually moves, and adjustments need to be made with your footwork, body position, and technique execution.

Striker basics

Start by assuming the on-guard position, ready to respond to the catcher's commands. Stand slightly more than a jab's length away from the catcher and be prepared to throw the requested punches and kicks. Stay alert and be ready to move in and out as you throw your combinations. Remain on-balance, and light on your feet while throwing with proper technique, accuracy, and speed.

Call and catch method

The catcher 'calls' out specific punches and combinations. The striker responds. This style of focus pad training allows for improvements in technique and building basic and more advanced combinations.

Start with catching and receiving the basic single punches using the following number sequencing:

1. Jab
2. Cross
3. Lead hook
4. Rear uppercut

1. Jab.

2. Cross.

3. Hook.

4. Uppercut.

Catcher calls 1: striker executes a jab.

Catcher calls 2: striker executes a cross.

Catcher calls 1-2: striker executes a jab–cross combination.

Catcher calls 1-2-3: striker executes a jab–cross–lead hook combination.

Catcher calls 1-2-3-4: striker executes a jab–cross–lead hook–rear uppercut combination.

As with all Kickboxing techniques, these basic punch combinations are the same when performed in the southpaw stance; they're simply 'mirrored' when compared to the orthodox stance.

1. Jab.

2. Cross.

3. Hook.

4. Uppercut.

DEFENSIVE MOVES

Skilful Kickboxers utilize defensive moves such as blocking, parrying, slipping and bobbing and weaving. We will be focusing on two important defensive tactics: slipping and bobbing and weaving in order to add a sense of realism to your workout.

Slipping

Focus pad training is the perfect tool to master the slipping motion since the catcher is simulating throwing a punch towards you. When executed properly, slipping moves work your leg and core muscles. Your previous training of visualizing punches coming at you and slipping while shadowboxing, hitting the heavy bag, and double-end bag will prepare you for slipping when training with the focus pads. Stay focused and react quickly when practising slipping. Always keep the hands up in the on-guard position and rotate your upper body, allowing the punch to go over your shoulder.

Slip to the *outside* of a given punch. Slip straight left punches over your left shoulder and straight rights over your right shoulder, regardless of your stance. Do not drop your hands and do not look at the floor. Keep your eyes on your partner at all times.

When the catcher simulates throwing a straight right or left, it is executed slowly, with minimal intent. The catcher must give the puncher sufficient time to slip out of the way.

Slipping a jab

The head, body, and shoulders move as one unit to the *outside* of the punch – if you're both in the orthodox stance, you will avoid your partner's left jab by slipping to the left. If you're both in the southpaw stance, avoid your partner's right jab by slipping to the left. Keep your body weight forward and stay off your heels, as the tendency is to lean back on the trailing foot.

Slipping a jab.

Slipping a cross

Dip to the outside of the punch, moving your head, shoulder and body together. Always return to your balanced fighting stance, hands by the face, and eyes on the catcher.

Slipping a cross.

Basic slipping combination 1

One-two – slip – slip

The puncher starts by throwing a one-two (jab followed by a cross) at the catcher's focus pads. The catcher immediately responds by simulating a jab and cross aiming for the striker's shoulder region. These moves from the catcher should be light and controlled. To avoid the incoming lead pad, the puncher slips to the right and then immediately slips to the left to avoid the catcher's incoming right and

1. Jab.

2. Cross.

3. Slip jab.

1. Slip jab.

4. Slip cross.

2. Slip cross.

left punch pads. Develop a smooth rhythm moving side-to-side with your hands held high, while holding your body core muscles firm.

As explained before, slipping is the same fundamental movement pattern from the southpaw stance as it is in the orthodox stance. Because the catcher always mimics the stance of the striker, James slips to his left, outside of Dan's right jab, and then to his right, outside of Dan's left cross.

Basic slipping combination 2

One-two – slip – cross – lead leg roundhouse kick

The striker starts by throwing a one-two (jab followed by a cross) at the catcher's pads. The

1. Jab.

2. Cross.

3. Slip jab.

4. Cross.

5. Step.

6. Lead roundhouse.

catcher immediately responds by simulating a jab aiming for the puncher's face. These moves from the catcher should be light and controlled. To avoid the incoming pad, the striker slips to the outside of the jab. Immediately counter with a cross at face level and step up with your rear foot to throw a lead leg roundhouse kick to the body.

Keys to Success

- Always keep your eyes on your partner, whether you are catching or punching.
- Avoid over slipping. This is when the slip is over-exaggerated and you are leaning too far to the right or to the left, leaving you off-balance.
- Keep your body weight centred through the balls of your feet. Never sit back on your heels.
- Ensure to keep your hands up high in the on-guard position. A common mistake is to drop your hands out of position when you shift your body weight from side-to-side.

Bobbing and weaving.

Bobbing and weaving

Kickboxers generally use a weaving motion to move under and avoid looping punches such as hooks.

Quickly bend the knees, lowering the head and dropping the body so the punch pad goes over the top of your head. This is the 'bobbing' part of the movement; bending your knees and getting down low.

When the catcher simulates a lead hook, the striker dips down under the hook and 'weaves' over to the other side to avoid the punch. When the catcher simulates a rear hook, the striker dips down and weaves over to the opposite side to avoid the punch. When you weave, bend your knees, keep your hands up, your chin down and *always* keep your eyes on the catcher. Do not bend the body forward to avoid the punch, just bend your legs. Always return to your on-guard position quickly.

To start, the catcher throws hooks slowly and high enough for the striker to duck underneath. As the striker becomes more proficient, the catcher can increase the speed of the hooks and lower the height of the hook to a more realistic head-level.

Basic bobbing and weaving combination 1

One-two – bob and weave – cross

The striker launches a one-two combination at the focus pads. The catcher returns with a simulated lead hook. To avoid the hook, the striker bends both legs and weaves under the hook,

1. Jab.

2. Cross.

3. Bob.

4. Weave.

5. Cross.

moving to the side, and then follows up by throwing a cross. The striker must always stay focused when manoeuvring under the focus pads. The catcher needs to simulate the hook in a controlled manner allowing the puncher to duck underneath. As the timing of the punches and the ducking becomes accurate, increase the tempo of this drill.

Basic bobbing and weaving combination 2
One-two – bob and weave – cross – lead leg roundhouse kick

The striker begins with a one-two combination at the focus pads. The catcher returns with a simulated lead hook. To avoid the hook, the striker bends both legs and weaves under the hook and then follows up by throwing a cross at face level and stepping up with the rear foot to throw a lead leg roundhouse kick to the body. As before, increase the tempo of this drill as it becomes more natural and 'flowing'.

1. Jab.

2. Cross.

3. Bob.

4. Weave.

5. Cross.

6. Step.

7. Lead roundhouse.

Keys to Success

- Always keep your eyes on your partner before, during, and after any combination.
- Focus on bending the legs to lower the body. Bending forward at the waist puts you off balance, increases strain on the lower back, and prohibits eye contact.
- Bend your knees just enough to manoeuvre under the focus pad.
- Practise the weaving motion while you are shadowboxing in front of a mirror.

BUILDING PUNCH COMBINATIONS

The following punch combinations and drills are broken down into easy-to-follow steps. Incorporate these combinations into your workout. Remember to continually communicate with your partner while throwing and catching.

Building combinations.

Combination 1

Jab – slip – cross – lead hook

The striker throws a jab to the catcher's lead focus pad. The catcher immediately comes back with a jab, tapping the striker on the

1. Jab.

2. Slip jab.

3. Cross.

4. Lead hook.

left shoulder. The striker quickly slips to the right, pivots back with a cross and finishes off with a lead hook. Be ready to move quickly.

Combination 2

One-two – slip – cross – hook – cross

The striker starts this drill with a quick one-two combination. The catcher simulates a jab as the puncher slips to the outside to avoid the incoming jab. The striker counters with three straight punches: cross – hook – cross. (Remember to keep your hands up when slipping.)

1. Jab.

2. Cross.

3. Slip jab.

4. Cross.

5. Lead hook.

6. Cross.

Combination 3

One-two – one-two – slip – slip – lead hook – cross

The striker throws four straight punches: lead – rear – lead – rear. The striker slips the catcher's lead and rear pad. The striker finishes with a lead hook and a cross. (When simulating the lead and rear punches, the catcher taps the puncher's lead and rear shoulders.)

1. One.

2. Two.

3. One.

4. Two.

5. Slip jab.

6. Slip cross.

7. Lead hook.

1. Jab.

8. Cross.

2. Cross.

Combination 4

1-2-3 – bob and weave – lead hook – cross

The striker starts by throwing a three-punch combination: jab, cross, and hook. The catcher simulates a rear hook over their partner's head while the striker ducks under the hook. The striker returns with a lead hook and a cross at the pads. (Stay focused when weaving, eyes on the target and weight on the balls of your feet.)

3. Hook.

4. Weave A.

5. Weave B.

6. Lead hook.

7. Cross.

BUILDING PUNCH-KICK COMBINATIONS

A consistent trait of skilled Kickboxers is their ability to combine punches and kicks in seamless combinations. The best Kickboxers can 'Box with their feet' as well as their hands. After getting a feel for the punch combinations, begin working on these punch-kick combinations.

Combination 1

Jab – jab – cross – lead leg roundhouse kick

The striker moves forward at an angle while executing a jab. Continue stepping forward at

1. Jab.

2. Second jab.

3. Cross.

4. Step.

5. Lead roundhouse.

an angle as the second jab is launched. Follow with a cross from a balanced position. Slide the rear foot forward to throw a lead leg roundhouse kick to the body. (The catcher must synchronize their movement with the striker. In this case, the catcher moves backward with each technique.)

Combination 2

Jab – rear uppercut – lead hook – rear leg roundhouse kick

The striker steps in with the jab. Follow up with a rear uppercut to the chin. Continue with a lead hook to the jaw. Launch a rear leg roundhouse kick to the head.

1. Jab.

2. Rear uppercut.

3. Lead hook.

4. Rear roundhouse.

1. Jab.

2. Cross.

3. Jab.

Combination 3

One-two-one – rear leg roundhouse – lead leg roundhouse – rear leg roundhouse

The striker steps in with the jab, followed by a cross, followed by another jab (1-2-1). As soon as the third punch lands, launch the rear leg roundhouse to the body. Step your foot down beneath the corresponding shoulder to follow up with a kick with the opposite (lead) leg.

4. Rear roundhouse.

5. Lead roundhouse.

6. Rear roundhouse.

Add a third (rear) kick to the sequence. Draw your rear leg back to your stance with your hands up.

Combination 4

Weave under rear hook – rear uppercut – lead hook – cross – lead leg roundhouse – rear leg roundhouse – double jab

Catcher throws a 'backhand' hook with the lead hand to simulate a rear hook. The striker weaves

1. Weave A.

2. Weave B.

3. Rear uppercut.

4. Lead hook.

5. Cross.

6. Step.

7. Lead roundhouse.

8. Step.

9. Rear roundhouse.

underneath the hook whilst simultaneously throwing a rear uppercut to the rear pad. The striker quickly follows up with a lead hook and a cross. The striker slides the rear foot forward to throw a lead leg roundhouse kick to the body. The striker steps the lead leg down after the roundhouse kick and immediately launches a follow-up roundhouse with the rear leg.

Free-style focus pads

Focus pad work creates a dynamic training environment that sharpens skills, reflexes, and develops form and power in your punches and kicks. When creating your own Kickboxing combinations, it should be both challenging and fun. Work the basic combinations until you become confident with them and then add more movement and increase your speed. After you have perfected your skills by working on the focus pad drills in this chapter, start to create your own combinations. When developing your own combinations, ensure they follow a logical sequence with each technique effectively setting up the next technique or movement.

Intensity

It is important to modify focus pad workouts to each individual's ability and skill level. This is accomplished by adapting the intensity level and the sequencing of the drills. The catcher sets the pace by allowing more or less time between techniques and movement.

5 LEARNING THE ROPES

To be a successful Kickboxer requires you to be as mentally tough as you are physically. The best Kickboxers train hard to master their hand–eye–foot coordination. It's essential to utilize all these elements at the same time when training or during combat. Jumping rope is one of the best ways to train your body to have all these elements working together.

Kickboxers utilize jump rope exercises as both a light warm-up and an intense 'cardio-finisher'. Out of all the exercises a Kickboxer can perform to imitate fighting footwork in the ring, nothing comes as close as jumping rope. It is one of the best aerobic workouts for Kickboxers, and it improves overall stamina.

Traditional jump rope techniques can be quite a challenge for some people to learn. Mastering jump rope requires lots of mental toughness. It is important to stay focused and in control, all the while concentrating on smooth footwork, balance, and timing. It takes time and commitment to master the basic jumps, but once this is accomplished, a wide variety of combinations can be performed. This not only makes the workout fun, but it also challenges a large variety of muscles. It works the gluteals, quadriceps, calves, and hamstrings. The upper body, the back and chest muscles, deltoids, forearms, biceps, and triceps are recruited to produce the movement of rotating and stabilizing the rope. To maintain proper alignment and the correct centre of gravity, the abdominal muscles are recruited to contract and hold the body position. Jumping rope challenges the cardiovascular system and improves coordination, which in turn helps to develop boxing agility, timing, power, and speed. It's a great total-body workout to improve over-all conditioning. Jumping rope will help you 'float like a butterfly and sting like a bee.'

The greatest Boxer of all time, Muhammad Ali, would dazzle his opponents with his fancy footwork, then throw a barrage of lightning-fast punches. Ali would dance around the ring and shuffle, rapidly alternating his feet front and back. If you ever had the opportunity to watch him shuffling his feet while jumping rope, keeping time, moving smoothly, you understand how he was so successful when he danced across the canvas during a fight.

OPPOSITE: **Learning the ropes.**

Bruce Lee was an outspoken advocate of jumping rope for cardiovascular fitness, touting its benefits in his book (published posthumously) *Bruce Lee's Fighting Method.*

EQUIPMENT

There are a variety of ropes to choose from, including plastic, beaded, and leather. A rope that is too long or too short will force you to adjust the position of the arms, causing poor execution of movement and jumping technique. A plastic segmented or 'beaded' jump rope allows for the length to be adjusted, customizing it specifically for the height that is required. A rope that is too light will not hold a true arc, and it will become more easily tangled, and not be able to create a sufficient amount of momentum to produce the desired motion. Conversely, a rope that is too heavy produces slow, cumbersome rotations, increases the risk of injury at the wrists and shoulders, and increases pain on impact when you miss. Look for a rope that has comfortable, durable, and well-constructed handles. The desired outcome of jumping is to develop cardiovascular fitness, fluidity, and agility. A rope that is too heavy or too light defeats this purpose and may take away from your ability to concentrate on proper jumping form and technique.

Select a rope that allows for a sufficient arc and does not place additional stress on the forearms and wrists. Also, choose a rope with handles that allow for easy rotation of the rope and fit comfortably into your hands.

Proper rope length

Using a rope that is the correct length will make it easier to execute your jumps. To decide which rope length is best for you, hold the handles of the rope in each hand and stand with one foot on the middle of the rope. Pull the rope up tight. The rope handles should reach the upper chest area.

FORM AND TECHNIQUE

Start with proper form and good technique. Whether you are just starting to jump or you are performing an array of masterful foot and arm movements, there are a few dos and don'ts.

- Jump only an inch or two off the ground.
- Keep the knees slightly bent.
- Land softly on the ground, rolling through the balls of the feet in order for the legs to absorb the impact.
- Keep the jumps in control with the torso upright. Do not allow the body to lean forward nor backward.
- Initiate the action of the turning of the rope at the wrist, with little movement at the shoulders or arms. (A proper weight of rope will assist in reduced shoulder and arm movement.)
- Keep the shoulders down and relaxed.
- Keep the arms at one level, with the upper part of the arm close to the sides of the body. Be careful not to allow the arms to drift away from the body, as this will raise the rope further from the floor and closer to the jumping feet, resulting in the rope becoming entangled in the feet.
- Keep the head in a neutral position and the neck relaxed.

It does take practice and practice pays off. Within a few weeks you will be putting together foot and arms combinations that will improve your agility, balance, and cardiovascular abilities.

The best surface to jump on is a gym, sprung wood floor as this reduces stress on the legs and feet.

JUMP ROPE PROGRESSIONS

Basic, intermediate, and advanced jumps are described below. With each training session, you will notice that your timing improves and you have more endurance. Continue to work on the basic jumps and then try adding some new combinations.

Basic jumps

Boxer's skip

Boxer's skip.

The Boxer's skip involves shifting your weight slightly from one foot to the other with each jump. The shift in weight is subtle as both feet are still making contact with the floor. You can perform a single bounce (right foot, left foot) or a double bounce (two rights, two lefts). This is a move up from the basic two-foot jump and lays the groundwork for more difficult jumps. Relax the shoulders and neck and remember to jump just a few centimetres off the floor.

Kick-step

The kick-step involves a slight kick forward alternating with each leg. Start with the boxer's skip, lift the right foot slightly backward and then perform a small kick forward. After the kick, land on the right foot. Now, lift the left foot slightly backward and kick it forward, landing on the left foot. Alternate the kicking legs and increase the difficulty by travelling forward and backward as you perform the kick-step.

Kick step.

Intermediate jumps

High knee jog

Similar to running on the spot, alternate lifting your knees high in front. Keep the body upright and the arms in the correct position. Land softly on the ground, using the feet, knees, and legs to absorb the impact. By lifting the knees high, the intensity level of the workout increases. Start this cardio interval training session by performing 8–10 high knee lifts and then take it down to a Boxer's skip to recover.

Repeat the high knee jog, increasing the numbers of knee lifts as you become more proficient. If you are trying to work this jump into your routine, you can add high knee lifts travelling forward and backward. This jump develops the muscle power in your legs and challenges your cardiovascular system.

High knees.

Boxer's shuffle.

The Boxer's shuffle

The Boxer's shuffle pays tribute to the classic Muhammad Ali foot movement utilized to confuse opponents. While moving around the ring Ali would suddenly shuffle his feet forward and backward, and then throw an unexpected series of punches. Practising this jump will train you to stay light on your feet and ready for any directional changes. The shifting of your foot positioning will also challenge your balance skills.

This is how to perform a slightly slower version of the shuffle: jump in the air, moving one foot slightly forward and the other foot slightly backward, and then land on the floor with both feet at the same time. Push off the floor again, taking the front foot towards the back and the back foot towards the front. Land with both feet on the floor alternating your feet constantly. Repeat, moving quickly and landing softly. Your agility and response time will be challenged due to the quick movement of the feet moving forward and backward. Complete 8–10 shuffles, then return to the Boxer's skip.

Jumping jacks

Jumping jacks are old-school calisthenics and can easily be worked into your rope training.

Jumping jacks.

As you jump, separate your feet shoulder-width apart. Land softly through the feet and then jump again bringing the feet together to land. Repeat. When performing this jump, be careful not to make the foot separation too wide as the rope will most likely get tangled with your feet. Start out with 6–8 jumping jacks and increase the number as you become more proficient.

Advanced jumps

Double jumps

To perform double jumps, jump high enough to allow two rotations of the rope while you are in the air. The rope speed must be faster and the jump must be substantially higher than the basic jump. Set your rhythm by performing a few basic two-foot jumps or Boxer's skips, and then perform a magnified jump with two fast rotations of the rope. As your timing and your fitness level improve, reduce the number of basic jumps in between your double jumps. This demanding jump requires more leg power and increased rope speed to be successful. Double jumps (or double hops) will improve your cardio-fitness and muscular endurance. Try to perform 6 double jumps, working your way up to 15.

Crossovers

Perform a basic jump at a comfortable pace. When the rope is overhead and moving forward, cross your arms at waist level and jump through the rope. When crossing the arms keep the handles by the sides of the body with the left handle at the right hip and the right handle at the left hip. The second time the rope comes overhead uncross the arms and jump through the rope once again. Keep the rope handles pointing out to the sides and not downward. When you perform the arm crossover motion you will have to jump slightly higher than the basic jump. Try to complete 3–4 front rope-cross jumps interspersed with a few basic jumps or Boxer's skips in between. Work up to 8–10 front crossovers in a row. This jump is also a front rope-cross.

Double jumps.

Crossover A.

Crossover B.

Crossover C.

Freestyle jumping

Your goal is to jump in a freestyle manner, incorporating a wide variety of moves and foot patterns into your skipping routine. Develop a smooth rhythm. There are countless jump

Freestyle jump rope.

patterns you can perform, but to get there you need to focus on the basics. Work the fundamentals before trying more complicated jumps and then use the neutral move to develop your new combinations. No matter how long you decide to jump, make it fun and challenging.

Jump rope sprints

This is an advanced interval routine, placing demands on your shoulders, core muscles, arms, and the cardiovascular system. Skip as fast as you can for short, timed intervals.

Option 1

Jump as fast as possible for 30 seconds and then rest for 30 seconds. Repeat for 10 to 15 sets. This drill should take you approximately 15 minutes to complete 15 sets. During the rest phase, walk around, keep moving, and catch your breath. To make this drill more challenging, jump as fast as possible for 30 seconds and reduce the rest time between sprints.

Option 2

Perform a 30-second sprint followed by jumping with the rope at a lower intensity for 30 seconds. Repeat for 6 to 10 sets.

It is best to choose a simple foot pattern you are comfortable with and can perform at a very fast pace. Once you become more proficient with the simple jumps, incorporate more challenging moves like crossovers or double jumps for your sprints.

Jump rope ladders

This interval drill helps to build your jumping stamina. Choose a number of jumps to start. For example, set a goal of 400 jumps, maintaining a consistent jumping pace. Take a 30–60-second rest. Reduce the number of jumps by 50 for each set. For your next ladder jump 350 times, then take a 30–60-second rest. Continue the down ladder to 50 jumps, taking 30–60-second rests in between. During the rest periods keep moving around.

JUMP	REST
400	30–60 seconds
350	30–60 seconds
300	30–60 seconds
250	30–60 seconds
200	30–60 seconds
150	30–60 seconds
100	30–60 seconds
50	30–60 seconds

Jump with intensity.

The total number of jumps you will perform is 1,800 for the 8 sets. This should take about 14 minutes if you are resting for 30 seconds and about 18 minutes to complete if you are resting for a full minute. To increase difficulty, take shorter rest periods between the sets or choose a higher starting number. Initially you may want to start your ladder at 300 jumps and reduce by 50 jumps each set, to the last 50 jumps.

KEYS TO SUCCESS

- Select the correct length of rope for your height.
- Perform one jump for each rotation of the rope.
- Ensure the rotation of the rope is moving at a constant speed.
- When turning the rope keep the arms by the sides of your body.
- Perfect your foot timing by practising the basic jumps.
- Incorporate the neutral move when putting together new jump combinations.
- Move around. Kickboxers never stay in one place.

The speed of the rope rotations, your height, body type, fitness level, and experience will influence the number of jumps performed. A starting jumping pace is around 110–130 per minute, an intermediate jumping pace is between 130–150 per minute, and a more advanced pace is about 160–180 jumps per minute. Listen to motivating music, warm up thoroughly and just start jumping.

6 RUN LIKE A KICKBOXER

If I could do only one exercise to prepare for a Kickboxing match, I would run. It is that valuable to me.

Don 'The Dragon' Wilson, World Champion

A successful Kickboxer's training regimen needs to encompass all aspects of physical training, such as muscular strength and endurance, flexibility, technical skills, agility, power, balance, and cardiovascular conditioning. As the saying in the fight game goes, 'cardio is king'. Effective running improves the ability of the heart and lungs to adapt to the demands placed on the body during Kickboxing training and competition. Running develops the cardio-respiratory and vascular systems so you can 'go the distance' in a Full Contact Kickboxing match.

When old-school Boxing coaches talk about 'roadwork' they are referring to a 6–10km (4–6 mile) run. These runs play an important role in a Boxer or Kickboxer's training, but more elements are needed to optimize the benefits of running to a fighter. Because of the intermittent nature of Kickboxing (2-minute rounds with a 1-minute break, throwing combinations in bursts etc.), faster paced, higher intensity sprints also need to be included in your running schedule. Imitating the demands of multiple 2-minute rounds is essential and this is accomplished by performing running sprints and interval training. An intense fight requires an increased demand for oxygen to be delivered to the working muscles.

Why run?

If two equally skilled Kickboxers compete against each other, the fighter who is more dedicated to running will more often than not be the victor in the ring.

Even though most knockouts and stoppages are achieved by landing punches, it is your legs that get you in and out of range. Getting into position to land a punch or kick, or moving to evade an opponent's attacks, is almost impossible if your legs are not in top shape. Running builds endurance and promotes explosiveness in the ring. Massimo Brizi is constantly moving when he is in the ring: pivoting, springing forward, backward and moving laterally. Don Wilson, Curtis Bush, Rick Roufus and Paul Vizzio are other examples of great 'movers' in the ring. Today, Alessio

OPPOSITE: **Run like a Kickboxer.**

Crescentini is a champion worth watching to see impeccable ring movement throughout the course of a bout.

Richard Bustillo, noted Martial Arts master and student of Bruce Lee, describes what it was like running with Bruce:

> *Back when I was training with Bruce, there wasn't much talk of what they now call interval training. Bruce was already doing that before it became popular. And what he used to do, he'd be jogging for a while, and then he'd be sprinting, and then he'd jog; and then he'd run backward, and then he'd jog; he'd even do crossovers, bringing his left leg over his right – and then he'd jog. He ran backward for footwork and co-ordination because he realized that fighting is not just like jogging; sometimes you've got to turn fast and backpedal. That's how he applied it and that's how he ran. Man, it was a workout!*

Warm weather running.

CONSIDERATIONS

Footwear

Purchase a comfortable and functional pair of running shoes. When your foot strikes the ground, the force produced is many times that of your body weight, so ensure that the shoes have good heel support, sole cushioning, and mid-sole flexibility. Consider your body type, foot structure and the terrain you will be running on to assist in determining your shoe choice. Visit a store that has knowledgeable and trained staff, try on many different styles, and make an educated purchase.

Hot weather

It generally takes a few weeks for your body to adjust to a significant increase in temperature so reduce your intensity when training in hot and humid weather. Run during the coolest part of the day, early morning or in the evening, and stay out of the direct sunlight. This will depend on how your training programme is structured. Most Full Contact Kickboxers will start the morning with their run, and the rest of their training will follow later in the day.

Wear light-coloured, breathable fabrics that fit to allow for free and comfortable movement. Clothing is now made with moisture-transport capabilities that allow perspiration to evaporate away from the body, and with UV protection built into the fabric. Protect your eyes from UV rays with non-slip sunglasses and wear a hat or bandana for cooling and UV protection benefits.

Ensure you are well hydrated, consuming water before, during and after exercising. Consuming 2–3 litres (8–12 cups) of water a day is normal for an active person, and aim to drink 120–180ml (½–¾ cup) of fluid in 20-minute intervals during your run. Sports drinks that replenish the electrolyte balance in your body may be a good choice when training for an extended period of time (over 60 minutes) and if it is extremely hot.

Cold weather

Winter running.

Do not train outside on extremely windy and icy days, or if the temperature is below –10 degrees Celsius or 15 degrees Fahrenheit. That would be a good opportunity to use a treadmill instead. To improve your footing on slippery roads, shorten your stride length, placing the foot on the ground and then lifting the foot during the push-off phase.

When running in cold weather, always dress in layers, ensure the head and hands are covered, and the face is protected. Start with a wicking base layer to keep your body dry and warm. Then layer with an insulating material, like fleece. This layer assists with the wicking of the moisture and also traps air close to the body to keep you warm. The third outer-layer made of wind-resistant and waterproof material protects against the wind and wet weather. Fifty per cent of body heat is lost through the head and even more if the hands are not covered. Wear a toque or balaclava on your head, gloves or mitts on your hands, and a covering over your mouth and nose to warm the air you are breathing. If the sun is shining wear sunscreen and high-quality UV sunglasses to protect your eyes against the reflection from the snow.

Meals

It is best to wait at least 90 minutes after eating a full meal before training, and the larger the meal, the longer you should wait before a long run. Working out too soon after a larger meal may cause an ineffective workout as the body is expending resources digesting food and not providing oxygen to the working muscles. If you run first thing in the morning, only a drink such as pure water or a preferred beverage such as coffee or tea is recommended before running.

Illness

Whether you get the flu with gastrointestinal symptoms or experience contraindications from a respiratory infection, it is best to rest until you have felt well for a full 24 hours. Recovering from an illness can take several weeks to regain strength, so it is important to adjust your training when you start back. If you are taking prescription or over-the-counter medications, always consult with your doctor or medical professional about returning to your training programme.

Pollution

If the pollution index is high, it may be best to train indoors to reduce the occurrence of respiratory issues.

TECHNIQUE

For a more successful running session and to help reduce the chance of injuries, start with the correct form and running technique.

General principles for effective running

- Look straight ahead, chin and head in a neutral position.
- Keep your shoulders relaxed.

Effective running technique.

- Keep your elbows bent at 90 degrees, letting the arms swing naturally forward and backward.
- Keep the fists relaxed and the hands partly open.
- Hold the body core muscles tight for back support and the hips with a slight tip upward.
- Avoid moving the knees up and down excessively. Move the knees in a smooth horizontal motion.
- Allow the foot to swing forward naturally, landing with the foot in front of the knee.
- Aim for a quick foot turnover, reducing the amount of contact time with the ground.
- Maintain a comfortable running style.

Uphill technique

- Shorten your stride-length, with the arms and legs synchronized.
- Keep the chest up and momentum forward as you lean into the hill.
- Keep the body weight forward onto the balls of the feet.
- Increase your effort as you run past the top of the hill.

Uphill technique.

Downhill technique

Downhill technique.

- Open your stride and keep your core muscles engaged.
- Maintain control as you let gravity pull you along.
- Concentrate on the running surface, watching for loose stones and slippery conditions.
- Maintain the proper foot placement and arm swing.

RUNNING AS A FIGHTER

Shadowboxing warm-up.

The Kickboxer's rule: 7-minute miles or faster

A general guide or 'rule' for your regular 4–6-mile runs has been in Boxing and Kickboxing for decades, and that is the '7-minute miles or faster' rule. This means running at a pace that results in completing every mile of your run in 7 minutes or less without stopping. So, a 4-mile run would take a maximum of 28 minutes. The 'rule of thumb' is that if you complete a mile in 7 minutes or less, you're running, not jogging.

Distance

When you are training for fights, you will be running between 4 and 6 six miles, six days per week. You will follow the '7-minute miles or faster' rule for your speed, and you'll also include sprints into these runs that are detailed later in this chapter. Once per week, you will replace one of these runs with an interval running session; there are two options for this once-per-week session, also detailed later in this chapter. Before you are ready to run as a fighter, you'll need to work up to this level of training.

Getting started with running

Begin your running regime with caution; it is important to gradually adapt to running rather than pushing yourself too much, too soon, and risking injuries. Start by running three mornings per week at a pace that you can sustain for 20 minutes. Don't worry about how fast or how far you are running at this stage; just complete your 20 minutes, three times a week. It's best to do this on alternating days, e.g., Monday, Wednesday, and Friday. This allows you to recover on your rest days and get used to running throughout the week. While following this schedule over a couple of months, you will adapt to regular running and be physically prepared to move towards your goal of 'maintenance running' four to five days per week at a 7-minute-mile pace.

When you're able to run 3 miles in 21 minutes or less, you know you're in shape.

Maintenance running

When you don't have a fight coming up, you should be within reaching distance of your peak conditioning. This is accomplished by maintaining the basic structure of your running schedule, but reducing the volume, intensity and frequency. Professional fighters can maintain their fitness by running 4–5 miles, four to five days per week. The intensity of your runs shouldn't be as high as when you're training to fight, but you should still challenge yourself. Remember, 7-minute miles or faster. While your 'running to fight' schedule includes sprints, you may decide to eliminate the sprints from your runs while you're in a 'maintenance running' phase and instead run the full distance at a constant pace.

Stay within 2–3kg (5–7lb) of your fighting weight at all times. This is also a great principle for lifelong health when you conclude your fighting career. This will be predominantly accomplished through a healthy, well-balanced and calorie-controlled approach to nutrition, but regular exercise will help towards that goal.

Running to fight

When you have a fight confirmed, it's time to step up your game. You'll be running six days per week in preparation for your fight. Many fighters prefer to run in the morning and go to the gym later in the day or the evening, but some prefer to train in the morning and run at night. Whichever schedule you prefer, stick to it for the duration of your fight training.

To succeed as a professional fighter, your legs have to be in top shape. Run between 4 and 6 miles. These runs are to be performed at a 7-minute-mile pace at least, before the last several minutes are focused on sprints. To lay out the structure for one of these runs,

Running to fight.

begin by deciding on the total distance that you will run, e.g., 4 miles. Run the first 3.5 miles at your regular pace and then stop to catch your breath for 30–60 seconds. Then, perform a 30-second sprint at a fast pace that you can maintain for the entire sprint, and then rest again for a period of 30–60 seconds. Repeat this process a total of five times, which will likely take your total running distance to a little over 4 miles. Essentially, this run is 4 miles in distance and includes five 30-second sprints.

This 4-mile run can be replicated exactly on a treadmill. Set the speed to an approximate 7-minute-mile (or faster) pace, and run until you have completed 3.5 miles. You can increase or decrease the speed throughout this 'distance' part of the run, but keep your 7-minute-mile pace as your minimum speed. It's a good idea to increase your speed towards the completion of the distance to train yourself to fight hard at the end of a round or a contest. After completing 3.5 miles, hop off the conveyer belt, pause the treadmill and take deep breaths. Now you will perform your five, 30-second sprints. When you get back on the treadmill and un-pause it, set the speed to a level where you will be sprinting. Work

Treadmill training.

up towards sprinting at 11mph. Don't set the speed so fast that you risk disorientation and falling off the treadmill. If you need more intensity, increase the incline on the treadmill which simulates running uphill. You can increase the incline with each sprint for more challenge.

Try to rest for no more than 1 minute between the time you finish your distance run and begin your first sprint. Likewise, keep the rest periods at or under 1 minute between each sprint. By the time you get off the treadmill and pause it, catch your breath, un-pause the treadmill, and allow it to get back up to speed, the time can easily get away from you. You want to be back on the treadmill, sprinting, in no more than 1 minute from when you stopped. The goal is to train your heart rate to recover more and more quickly between the sprints. This simulates recovering during the 1-minute break between each round of hard fighting in the ring.

Whether running outdoors or on a treadmill, perform between five and ten sprints at the end of your regular runs. The 'distance' component should comprise the majority of your run while the sprints are a relatively brief segment at the end. Run at least 3.5 miles before you begin the sprints. If you're performing this run on an almost daily basis, as you should be, and your training schedule also includes other hard workouts, you will benefit

Interval running.

from limiting your sprints to five repetitions on *most* of these runs.

We recommend that you run slightly easier every other day, no matter where you are in your training schedule or proximity to a fight date. For example, on Monday, Wednesday and Friday, you may wish to increase your speed above your normal pace during the distance part of the run, and if you're on a treadmill, to raise the incline on your sprints to increase the challenge. On Tuesday, Thursday and Saturday, avoid these intensifiers; simply run at your normal speed (at least a 7-minute-mile pace) throughout the distance part of the run, and if using a treadmill, either forgo using an incline or keep the incline gradient low on your sprints. Your runs need to be sustainable enough that you can perform them consistently to reap the fitness benefits of regular running, but also to be able to recover from them to perform in your training session later in the day, and to do it all over again tomorrow. If you follow this approach, your ability to complete more distance at a faster pace will improve gradually and consistently over time.

Keys to Success

- Run between 4 and 6 miles (6–10km) total.
- Run at a 7-minute-mile pace or faster.
- Include 5–10 sprints of 30 seconds at the end of each run. 11mph is a good pace for sprints.
- Rest for no more than 1 minute between sprints.
- Run harder on one day and slightly easier the next day (minimum 7-minute miles). Continue alternating your runs in this fashion.
- Run six days per week: run in the morning and train later in the day.

INTERVAL RUN WORKOUTS

Perform one of these runs *only once* per week to substitute one of your standard runs. That means that you will perform either the first *or* the second interval run once during that particular week. Any more than this, in conjunction with the rest of your running and training, can easily lead to suppressed immunity to illness or injury.

It is recommended that you perform one of these interval runs, once per week, from between six to two weeks before your bout.

Sprints.

Before and after this designated time period, stick to your standard runs. Both your training and your rest have to be partitioned carefully during your preparation for a fight. You must recover from the stress imposed on your body in order for the training to be successful.

Interval run 1: 12 x quarter-mile intervals

If you choose this interval run, you will be running twelve repetitions of quarter-mile (400m) intervals at as fast a pace as you can sustain for all of the intervals. It is important to choose a realistic pace when attempting this run for the first several times, allowing your speed endurance to develop over the weeks. It is of no benefit to run the first quarter-mile in 1 minute and 30 seconds, and then finish the workout by completing the intervals in 2 minutes. The goal is to complete every interval at the same pace, if not improving on your lap times during the course of the workout.

After each interval, walk slowly and take deep breaths to recover before beginning your next interval. Try to limit your rest period to 1 minute. This replicates the amount of time you have to recover and rejuvenate between rounds of Kickboxing during a bout. When starting out, if you need more time, take it, but when you're a competitive professional, just as with your speed on each interval, keep your rest time consistent after each interval. Your goal is to eventually bring your rest time down to 1 minute and keep it there.

This workout is particularly suited to the track, although it can be replicated on a treadmill. Make sure to go through a thorough warm up before this interval session. Include a few minutes of jogging into your warm up, gradually increasing the pace to prepare yourself for the hard running ahead. Follow this with some pre-activity stretches to conclude your warm up. Remember, you would only perform this run once per week, so give it a concentrated effort because you will have to wait until the following week to go through this workout again. After completing this workout, walk for several minutes and stretch thoroughly to cool down (*see* Chapter 8).

Keys to Success

- Run 12 quarter-mile (400-metre) intervals in total.
- Set as fast a pace as you can that you will be able to sustain for every interval.
- Rest for 1 minute between each interval by walking slowly and drawing breath.
- Warm up and cool down thoroughly, taking care to avoid potential injury.

Interval run 2: 'Fifteen rounds of running'

If you choose this second interval run *instead* of the previous run, you will be running fifteen intervals of 2 minutes with a 1-minute rest period between each interval. This replicates the exact amount of time per interval as you would fight during a round in a Full Contact Kickboxing match. When fighting in the ring, your intensity level and thus your heart rate would vary. There would be times that you would fight hard, throwing combinations, and times where you would move around the ring and take some deep breaths. This run requires you to sustain a constant pace for the full 2 minutes of each interval, and then repeat the same sustained pace after a 1-minute break. This is to be repeated for a total of fifteen intervals or rounds.

As in the case of the first interval run, choose a pace for your 'fifteen rounds of running' that is as fast as you can sustain for

2 minutes, and can repeat fifteen times. This may take some trial and error. If you have a good fitness level, you won't be running quite as fast as during the quarter-mile intervals, because the quarter-mile intervals would take you less than 2 minutes each to complete. But these 2-minute intervals will require you to run for the exact same amount of time for every interval; you can't cut it short by running a little harder. If you run quarter-mile intervals at a 10mph pace, then a good pace for your 2-minute intervals would be 9–9.5mph. As with the previous interval run, walk for several minutes after completing the workout and stretch thoroughly.

Keys to Success

- Run fifteen 2-minute intervals in total.
- Set as fast a pace as you can that you will be able to sustain for every interval.
- Rest for one minute between each interval by walking slowly and drawing breath.
- Warm up and cool down thoroughly, taking care to avoid potential injury (*see* Chapter 8).

Starting out.

A FINAL WORD ON RUNNING

As you have read in this chapter, running is an integral part of a Kickboxer's training programme. While the general guidance in this chapter should be followed to ensure the necessary conditioning for fighting, you may identify the need to modify the running methods in this guide to accommodate your requirements and schedule. With the help of your coaches, you can make sound judgement on how to design the most effective running schedule for *you*. For a running programme to be effective, it must provide you with the necessary conditioning; that's the ultimate goal. Some fighters may need more running volume (miles) and frequency (number of runs) to accomplish this, while others would find themselves in an overtrained state if they attempted such a schedule in combination with their gym training. This will take some trial and error on your part to find the 'sweet spot' amount of running that you require, at various key points throughout your training for a bout (e.g. a two-month preparation) that coincides with your gym work to get you in the best condition possible to step into the ring.

> *I was running 6 to 7 miles a day for my first world title crack back in 1986, but I lost and felt 'spent' the entire fight. Before and after that fight, I only ran 4 miles a day for fights. That's when I felt strong.*
>
> *Curtis Bush, World Champion*

COMBAT
SYSTEM EVOLUTION
IKTA

7 WEIGHT TRAINING FOR KICKBOXING

MUSCLE CONDITIONING

Some 'old-school' Boxing trainers believed that weight training should not be part of a fighter's workout regimen. It was felt that weight training would produce a muscle-bound, slower moving fighter in the ring and that bag work, roadwork, and sparring were sufficient training to increase speed and punching power. The fact is that weight training better prepares you for battle in the ring. It puts power into the punches and stability into the stance, and it reduces the occurrences of joint and muscle injuries. Weight training increases overall stamina, punching and kicking speed, and lean body mass. Strength training is essential to the whole training package, complementing the overall outcome.

The most effective training routine places emphasis on using weights to supplement the overall workout programme, promoting improved capabilities for your Kickboxing training. The programme encourages muscular strength and endurance, which in turn provide the basis for stronger and more powerful punches and kicks. Improvements in speed, technique, agility and response time will result from lifting weights.

OPPOSITE: Resistance training.

With specific training, the muscles learn how to respond faster and more efficiently and effectively to specific demands. With continual repetition of a movement, the muscle fibre instinctively performs the movement requested. When we perform and demand the very best and the very extreme from each movement, the muscle fibre increases in strength and circumference with an improved outcome – greater muscle efficiency.

The Muscle Conditioning Programme: the 10-rep max

Traditionally, when training with weights, eight to twelve repetitions of an exercise are performed, and this is repeated three times. Our goal is to provide a programme that will give you strength gains in the least amount of time. The method of weight training used here will be based on lifting a specified weight a maximum of ten times in the second set of the exercise routine, while the eleventh lift cannot be completed.

In the first set, the goal is to lift the weight more than ten repetitions (around twelve repetitions). This is usually around 75–80% of the weight used for the 10-rep max. In the second set, the weight is increased so that the muscle will fatigue at ten repetitions. In the third set, the weight is reduced to the same weight as used in the first set, and the weight is lifted as many times as possible until total muscle fatigue results.

If you have trained with weights previously, it should be easy to determine your 10-rep max. If you are new to weight training, start with a lighter weight, perhaps lifting the weight twelve to fourteen repetitions. If you are able to complete eleven reps or more, then you know you will need a heavier weight for the next set. If, on the other hand you cannot complete a set of ten repetitions, the weight is too heavy and for the next set the poundage should be reduced. It may take two or three workouts (one to two weeks), to determine your exact 10-rep max. It is always better to find your 1-rep max by lifting a lighter weight and placing stress on the muscle fibre by increasing the number of repetitions than by trying to lift a weight that you cannot even push eight times. The risk of injury increases, especially to the connecting tissues (ligaments and tendons).

By causing the muscle to go to failure (unable to perform the lift), stress or an overload has been placed on the muscle fibres. The waste material, lactic acid, inhibits the muscle contractile system to respond to the requested work. It will take the lactic acid 30 to 45 seconds to break up, and then the exercise can be repeated. Muscles adapt to the added weight/stress and will perform at a greater weight after they have repaired (usually 24 to 48 hours).

First set: 80% of 10-rep max (12 to 14 repetitions)
Second set: 100% of 10-rep max (10 repetitions)
Third set: 80% of 10-rep max (repetitions to fatigue)

Order of exercises

The exercises should be performed in the order that they are listed, from the largest muscle group to the smallest ones. It is important to work the larger muscles first, as the smaller muscles are required for stability. The smaller muscle is the weak link. When the larger muscles are worked, the smaller muscles assist in the movement for the larger muscles. For example, the bench press requires the use of the chest muscles, and the triceps muscle assists in the lifting movement. If the triceps are fatigued, the pectoral muscles will not execute the movement properly and inhibit the development of the chest.

Weight equipment

Weight machines are utilized for this training routine. The use of weight machines with cable systems or self-spotting devices allows you to perform an exercise to muscle failure if you are working out on your own. The weight equipment at any gym should be studied, and choices should be made according to availability of a spotting partner, the fit of the machine to your body frame and the intended outcome of the exercise.

When lifting, body-position, the execution of the exercise, and breathing are important elements to remember. Exhale on effort, or when pressing the weight away from the starting position, and inhale on relaxation, or when returning the weight back to the starting position. Find a comfortable rate of execution. It should not be too quick, because the momentum of the weight, not your muscle power, will be carrying the limb to the end position. Try to take the weight through the full range of motion, engaging a broad array of muscle fibres. Move the weight from the starting position in a controlled manner, pause and then back again to the finish position. The movement is smooth and controlled. It is important to keep the body in the correct position as shown in the photographs. The core is held tight, and all posture and supporting muscles are in alignment so the exercise may be executed correctly. This also reduces chance of injury in the working muscle as well as supporting muscles and joint regions.

Some considerations

The weight that you are able to lift may vary from workout to workout. Some days you may feel stronger and be able to press more weight; other days you may feel fatigued before you even start. Extraneous conditions (such as health and personal commitments) can influence your workout capabilities. A reduced ability in lifting weights is often noticed during your first set. If during your first set you struggled to get 10 reps or did not even get 10 reps, reduce the weight for the second set. Do not forgo your workout; try to keep your schedule; just reduce the intensity of the workout.

Bench press start.

EXERCISES WITH WEIGHTS

Perform the exercises in the following order. Rest for 1–2 minutes between each set and each exercise.

Bench press

Targeted muscles: pectoralis major, serratus anterior

Lie on your back on an incline flat bench, set at an angle less than 60 degrees. Elbows bent at a right angle with respect to the upper arm, hold the dumbbells in an overhand grip. Inhale and press the weights away from the chest, extending the arms until the weights touch softly. Exhale and slowly lower the weights towards the chest.

Bench press finish.

Lat pull-down

Targeted muscles: latissimus dorsi, teres major

Sit facing the weight machine. Hold the bar in an overhand wide grip, arms extended. Sit tall, leaning slightly back, chest lifted forward, and knees steadied under the leg pads. Inhale and pull the bar down on an angle towards the upper chest. Squeeze the shoulder blades together by bringing the elbows back as you pull through. Pause and exhale, returning the bar to the starting position slowly and with control.

Lat pulldown start.

Lat pulldown finish.

Seated pec deck

Targeted muscles: pectoralis major, serratus anterior

Sit with the arms out at right angles (bent up at the elbows) at shoulder level and the forearms placed on the pads of the weight machine. Keep the back straight, shoulders relaxed and look straight ahead. Bring the arms together, contracting the centre of the chest, and pulling from the elbow area, until the pads come together. Pause and return the pads to the starting position. Exhale as the arms are

Seated pec deck start.

Seated pec deck finish.

brought together, and inhale as the arms open up towards the sides.

Seated row

Targeted muscles: latissimus dorsi, rhomboideus

Sit with your knees slightly bent and your feet braced for support. Grasp the handles, and then pull your elbows straight back. Maintain a strong torso, while bringing the shoulder blades towards the centre line of your body. Pause and then slowly release to the starting position. Exhale as you pull back and inhale as you return to the starting position.

Seated row start.

Seated row finish.

Seated shoulder press

Targeted muscles: anterior/medial deltoid

Sit with your feet flat to the floor, back straight and torso held tight. Hold the bar in an overhand grip, exhale as you press the bar overhead. Maintain a strong torso throughout while

Shoulder press start.

Shoulder press finish.

executing the movement from the shoulder region. Pause at the top and then lower to the start position with control, inhaling.

Biceps curl

Targeted muscles: biceps brachii

Stand with feet hip-width apart, the abdominals held tight, and the arms slightly bent at the elbow to maintain tension on the muscle. Extend the arms close to the sides of the body. Hold the weights in an underhand grip, knuckles facing either forward or in towards the body. Keeping the torso strong and the elbows close to the body, raise the weights up towards the chest area. Pause at the top and lower the weights to the starting position, stopping in front of the thighs.

Biceps curl start.

Biceps curl finish.

Triceps pull-down

Targeted muscles: triceps brachii, teres major, teres minor

Stand, facing the machine. Hold the bar with both hands in an overhand close grip, chest level. Place the feet slightly less than hip-width apart, knees relaxed and torso tight. Keep the elbows close to the body and press the bar down towards the upper

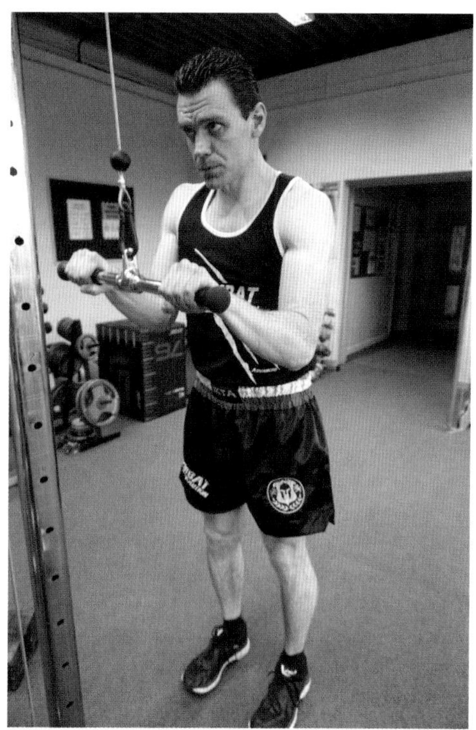

Triceps pulldown start.

Triceps pulldown finish.

Leg press start.

thighs until the arms are extended. Pause and slowly return the bar to the starting position, keeping the elbows at the sides of the body. Exhale as you press the bar down, and inhale as you release the bar.

Leg press

Adjust the seat so the knees are bent at 90 degrees. Place the feet shoulder width apart. Slowly extend the legs but don't lock the knees. Return to the starting position with slow, controlled movement.

Leg press finish.

Leg extension

Targeted muscles: quadriceps, rectus femoris, vastus medialis, lateralis and intermedius

Sit tall on the bench with the back supported and the thighs fully on the bench. Contract the

Leg extension start.

Leg extension finish.

quadriceps muscles and raise the lower legs slowly until they are extended. Pause at the top and then lower the legs slowly to the starting position. Perform with a controlled movement. Do not kick or swing the legs up. Do not allow the momentum of the weight to move the legs. Exhale on lifting the legs, and inhale on lowering the legs.

Hamstring curls

Targeted muscles: biceps femoris (long and short head), gastrocnemius

Sit on the bench with the legs extended and the back of the ankle on the pads. Contract the torso muscles and slowly pull the lower legs down towards the floor. Pause and then return the legs to the start position.

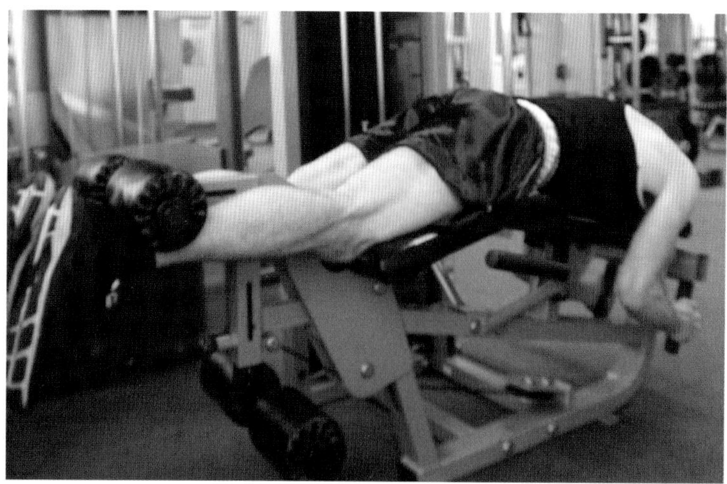

Hamstring curl start.

Hamstring curl finish.

Abdominal exercise: sit-ups

Sit-ups work the entire abdomen, providing core strength and endurance, as well as developing a rock-solid musculature capable of withstanding blows to the body. Perform a full sit-up; keep tension on the abdominals by only lightly touching the floor or pad with your back, before sitting up again. You can add a twist to alternating sides which will bring more of your rotational muscles into the exercise. Sit-ups can be performed as part of your weight training workout, as part of your Kickboxing workout or after your morning run. Perform 200 daily sit-ups when training for a fight; you can break these up into 8 sets of 25 repetitions, or 4 sets of 50 repetitions.

Sit-ups with a medicine ball for added resistance.

8 STRETCHING AND FLEXIBILITY FOR KICKBOXING

The explosive nature of Kickboxing requires an extreme range of motion for many of the kicks and punches. Kickboxing requires a high level of flexibility, and it is an essential component that will only enhance athletic performance. Optimal muscle length and joint mobility provide better coordination and muscle control, and allow for proper execution of striking movements.

Including a stretching session in all of your workouts gives you a sound and effective training programme. A regular stretching programme is essential to maintain the best possible conditioned and flexible musculature and the optimal range of motion at your joints.

Benefits of stretching.

BENEFITS OF STRETCHING

Flexible joints and muscles help to minimize the risk of injury. It is important that the muscles surrounding the joints are able to move through a full range of motion without placing undue strain on the ligaments, tendons, and capsular structures. When muscles are unable to extend all the way, you are increasing the risk of joint pain, strains and muscular damage. Also, strong muscles that are pliable and limber can withstand any additional stress resulting from intense training. A strong muscle that is rigid and inflexible will tear, resulting in soreness and discomfort.

OPPOSITE: Flexibility training for Kickboxing.

Stretching increases blood flow to the muscles and assists with improved circulation. Increased blood flow to the muscle tissues supplies essential nutrients to working muscles and helps to reduce muscle soreness. The more conditioned and subtle your muscles and tendons are, the better they can manage intense physical demands.

Stretching and flexibility promote the maintenance of good posture, assisting in a better quality of everyday life activities. As well, stretching can help the muscles relax and relieve any tension.

Reduction of muscle soreness

The lactic acid that builds up in the muscle tissue when you are working out will often cause soreness and fatigue in your muscles. By stretching these muscles, the blood circulation to that area is increased and this helps to flush out the lactic acid build-up. By lowering the occurrence of muscle soreness, you are more likely to stick with your workout schedule.

STRETCH EVERY DAY

For overall physical fitness, stretching needs to occur on a regular basis. Focus on the key areas that you are training and include more stretches for these areas. Be aware of the muscles that are tight and spend additional time stretching them. Often people will not stretch a muscle or joint area until they actually feel stiff or sore. Aim to find the balance between the strength of a muscle and the extensibility of that same muscle. Due to sport-specific demands, poor postural habits, or previous injuries muscular imbalance may be evident. Take the time to stretch the muscles that have become too tight or inflexible. Stretch both sides of your body, making sure that the range of motion and extensibility are as equal as possible on each side. It is most beneficial to perform stretching exercises at the end of your workout; you may be tired and less keen to do so and will forgo your stretching. Over a period of time this often leads to the muscles becoming less pliable and a reduced range of motion at your

Stretch every day.

joint areas. Stretch to keep both your mobility and independence and always make time to stretch with every workout.

TYPES OF FLEXIBILITY TRAINING

Static stretching

Static stretching exercises are safe and are used to increase the range of motion at a joint. Slowly stretch to the farthest point and hold the stretch. There should not be any pain associated with this stretch. The stretch is held for a brief period of time (30 to 60 seconds), and then released back to the starting muscle length.

Dynamic stretching

Dynamic stretching prepares the body for movement and is sport-specific. It combines both flexibility and strength, taking the muscle through a large range of motion and focusing on the movement patterns required for training. These exercises are performed in a controlled manner and at faster rate than static stretching. Do not bounce or force the stretch and hold the stretch for a very short period of time (5–10 seconds).

Passive stretching

Passive stretching is created by an external force, like a mechanical device, a partner, or gravity causing the muscle to stretch. The muscles around the joint remain inactive and relaxed.

Proprioceptive neuromuscular facilitation (PFN stretching)

PFN stretching, also called 'active assist stretching', increases range of motion and flexibility and originated as a rehabilitation technique. It is important to warm up the muscles before performing this type of stretching. To execute, lengthen a muscle close to its maximum level (static stretch), then contract the muscle in that lengthened state. This contraction is held for 10–20 seconds and then relaxed for 20 seconds. During the relaxation, slowly increase the stretch. Another hold–relax stretch is then performed.

Pre-activity stretching

The purpose of a pre-activity stretch is to warm-up the muscles and joint areas and not necessarily to increase the length of the muscle. Always warm up your muscles and joint areas before performing stretches by increasing your heart rate. This can be accomplished by walking around, performing large arm circles, and leg lifts, and imitating the training you will be doing later, for about 5 minutes. Perform dynamic stretches, taking the muscles through a large range of motion and reducing any tightness.

Post-activity stretching

As previously mentioned, it is extremely beneficial to stretch at the end of a workout. The purpose of a post-activity stretch is to lengthen the muscles you have been training. Stretching promotes blood flow to these muscles assisting in the removal of by-products such as lactic acid. Hold a post-activity stretch for 30–60 seconds, moving into the stretch until a mild tension is felt in the muscle; pause and then try to reach slightly further into the stretch. Perform static stretches, always moving gently and slowly into the stretch. If the stretch feels painful, then you have moved too far or too fast into the stretch. Release the stretch and hold where there is not any pain. Focus on the muscle you are trying to lengthen and do not place any stress on the associated joints. Never bounce or force a stretch, as this can cause small tears in the muscle fibres, resulting in pain and scar tissue. Always breathe during your stretch and never hold your breath. Breathe in as you prepare for the stretch and breathe out as you move into your stretch.

STRETCHES FROM HEAD TO TOE

Perform stretches for all of your muscle groups, spending additional time stretching the muscles you have trained hard and any muscles that feel tight.

Neck stretch

Targeted muscles: levator scapula, upper trapezius

Either sitting or standing, bend your head to one side and slightly forward. Place the opposite hand lightly on the side of your head, and gently pull downward. Hold the stretch for 30 seconds. Release and perform the stretch tilting your head to the other side.

Upper back and shoulder stretch

Targeted muscles: trapezius, rhomboid, teres minor, teres major, infraspinatus, posterior deltoid

To stretch the upper back, extend one arm and bring it in front of your body. Keep the shoulders square and relaxed, holding onto the elbow area with your other hand. Take a breath and as you exhale gently press the arm towards your body. Hold the stretch for 30 seconds. Release. Next, bend the arm at your elbow, inhale and then exhale, pressing the arm across your chest towards the other shoulder. Allow the shoulder to roll forward slightly. This stretches out the rear deltoid muscle of the shoulder. Hold the

Neck stretch – tilt your head to one side.

Neck stretch – gently stretch on the opposite side.

Upper back and shoulder stretch A.

Upper back and shoulder stretch B.

Pull back lat stretch.

stretch for 30 seconds. Release. Perform both stretches with the other arm.

Pull back lat stretch

Targeted muscles: latissimus dorsi, posterior deltoid, infraspinatus

Standing, grasp a secure object that is fixed to the floor or ground with both hands at approximately waist level. Breathe in, and then exhale as you sit back allowing the arms to fully extend, stretching through the latissimus dorsi and posterior deltoid. Try shifting your weight slightly to one side for a further stretch in the back region. Hold the stretch for 30 seconds breathing naturally.

Chest and shoulder stretch

Targeted muscles: pectoralis major, pectoralis minor, anterior deltoid

To stretch the chest and shoulder muscles, stand with your head facing straight forward and your neck and shoulders relaxed. Extend

Chest and shoulder stretch.

your arms behind your back and hold your hands together by interlacing the fingers. Inhale, pull the shoulder blades towards each other and lift the arms up slightly. Now exhale and lower the arms down slowly. Hold the stretch for 30 seconds.

Overhead triceps stretch

Targeted muscles: triceps, deltoid, rotator cuff

The triceps, deltoids, and rotator cuff are all stretched with this exercise. Both arms start in the overhead position. Look forward with the head in a frontal neutral position. Bend one arm back with the elbow pointing towards the ceiling. Try to place the palm of the hand or your fingers near the centre of your back, between the shoulder blades. Place your other hand on the elbow, breathe in and then as you breathe out, press down on the elbow slightly moving the hand down the back. Hold the stretch for 30 seconds. Release the stretch. Repeat on the other arm.

Overhead triceps stretch – back view.

Chest and biceps stretch

Targeted muscles: pectoralis major, pectoralis minor, biceps, rotator cuff, deltoids

Standing by a wall, place your bent arm at shoulder height against the wall. Breathe in, and then exhale slowly as you turn your body away from the wall. To target the upper chest muscles, place the arm further down on the

Overhead triceps stretch – front view.

Chest and biceps stretch – allow your muscles to relax completely.

wall, and to target the lower chest muscle, place your arm in a position that is slightly higher on the wall. Hold the stretch for 30–60 seconds. Release the stretch. Repeat on the other arm.

Kneeling forearm stretch

Targeted muscles: brachioradialis, palmaris longus, flexor carpi radialis

Kneeling with your arms directly positioned under your shoulders, press the palms of your hands into the ground with the fingers spread apart. Lift one hand and rotate it outward, keeping the fingers spread. Press your palm into the ground and circle your arm at the shoulder joint slowly in one direction for about 10 seconds and then change direction. Breathe normally. Release the stretch and repeat on the other arm. Alternate. This stretch may be executed while you are standing or sitting by holding onto the palm of one hand and lightly pressing backward. Hold the stretch for 30 seconds. Release the stretch. Repeat on the other arm.

Kneeling forearm stretch – arms directly under your shoulders.

Kneeling forearm stretch – press the palms of your hands into the ground.

Alternative standing forearm stretch.

Core side stretch

Targeted muscles: rectus abdominus, obliques, latissimus dorsi

Stand with the feet shoulder width apart, hipbones parallel to the ground, abdominal

Core side stretch – gently stretch to the side.

muscles held tight, and your knees slightly bent. Inhale, and then stretch your arm overhead, exhaling as you reach your arm in a semi-circle and bending your body to the side. Stretch from your fingertips right through to your hipbone. Breathe normally, holding the side stretch for 30–60 seconds. Take a breath in and then exhale, reaching up and returning to the start position. Repeat on the other side.

Lower back stretch

Targeted muscles: erector spinae, gluteals

To stretch your lower back and gluteal area, lie on your back with your knees bent and both feet on the ground. Breathe in, and then exhale as you pull both of your knees in towards your chest. Hold behind your knees. Hold the stretch for 30 seconds. Slowly release the legs and place both feet back on the floor. You can also vary the stretch by starting with both knees in by your chest, inhale and then as you exhale extend one leg long on the ground. Hold the stretch for 30 seconds. Bring both legs back to the chest and repeat with the other leg. To reduce the stress on your lower back, just pull one knee in towards the chest with your other foot on the floor.

Lower back stretch – pull both knees to your chest.

Lower back stretch – keep one knee by the chest as you extend your other leg.

Lower back stretch alternative position – keep one foot on the ground with bent knee.

Supine piriformis stretch

Targeted muscles: piriformis, gluteals, fascia lata

This stretch help prevents lower back tightening and tension. Start by lying on your back

Supine piriformis stretch – pull knees towards the chest.

with your knees bent and one foot on the ground. Place the ankle of the other leg on the bent knee. Lift both legs off the ground holding behind the thigh of the lower leg. Inhale and as you exhale, pull your legs in towards the chest. Breathe normally, holding the stretch for 30 seconds. Release and repeat on the other side.

Kneeling hip flexor stretch

Targeted muscles: hip flexors, quadriceps, groin

Kneeling hip flexor stretch – lightly press your hip forward.

To stretch a tight hip flexor muscle, place one knee on the ground and your opposite foot in front on the ground. Ensure that the front foot is positioned directly under the knee. The hip is bent at 90 degrees. Look forward with the head in a frontal neutral position and place both hands on your thigh, keeping your back straight. Inhale and as you breathe out, lightly press your hips forward. Hold the stretch for 30 seconds. Release and repeat on the other side.

Standing quadriceps stretch

Targeted muscles: quadriceps, rectus femoris

Standing quadriceps stretch – gently lift one foot backwards.

To stretch the front of your thigh, stand with your back and torso straight and thighs together. Lift one foot backward, keeping the knees close together. Take a breath in and hold onto your ankle. Exhale, pulling the heel up and towards your buttock. Hold this position for 30 seconds. Gently release and repeat on the other side.

ITB stretch (iliotibial band)

Targeted muscles: iliotibial band, tensor fascia lata

This thick band of connective tissue runs along the outer thigh, from the hip area to the knee. When it is not flexible and pliable, the knee joint may be pulled out of alignment and cause inflammation in your hip area. Stand and cross one foot over the opposite foot, keeping the knees soft or unlocked. Inhale bending at the waist and exhale as you reach

ITB stretch – exhale as you reach forward.

towards the floor. To increase the stretch, centre your weight through the rear leg. Hold this position for 30 seconds. Gently release and switch legs.

Lying hamstring stretch

Targeted muscles: hamstrings, erector spinae, gluteals

Start the hamstring stretch by lying on your back with both knees bent. Lift one leg and hold behind the thigh with both of your hands. Inhale and then exhale while you straighten the leg. Slowly pull the leg towards your body until a slight tension is felt in the hamstring muscle. Hold this position for 30 seconds. Gently release

Lying hamstring stretch – slowly pull your leg towards your body.

Lying hamstring stretch – for a deeper stretch, keep your legs extended.

and switch legs. For a deeper stretch, keep both legs extended long on the ground and lift one leg up and towards your body. Hold for 30 seconds and repeat on the other leg.

Standing calf/Achilles stretch

Targeted muscles: gastrocnemius, Achilles tendon

Stand with one leg forward and one leg back. Inhale and as you bend the front leg forward, exhale, keeping your rear leg straight and your rear heel on the ground. The stretch will be felt in the centre of the calf muscle. To stretch the lower area of the calf, bend your back knee slightly and shift your body weight back over the rear heel. This will stretch through the lower part of the gastrocnemius muscle and the Achilles tendon area of the leg. Hold each position for 30 seconds. Gently release and switch legs.

Standing calf–Achilles stretch – keep your heel on the ground.

Kneeling soleus–Achilles stretch.

Kneeling soleus/Achilles stretch

Targeted muscles: soleus, Achilles tendon

Start with one knee on the ground and the opposite foot placed on the ground beside your knee. Position your hands slightly in front of the knee on the ground to assist with balancing. Try to position your heel as close to the knee as possible. Take a breath in, and as you exhale, press your heel to the ground and shift your body weight forward slightly onto your hands. Hold this position for 30 seconds. Gently release and switch legs.

ADDUCTOR/HAMSTRING SPECIALIZED STRETCHING (PROGRESSIVE PROGRAMME)

Kickboxing requires overall flexibility, but the areas of the body that require exceptional flexibility in a Kickboxer are the adductor and the hamstring muscle groups of the legs. The adductor group is predominantly made up of three muscles on the inside of the thigh: the adductor longus, adductor brevis and adductor magnus, as well as the gracilis and the pectineus. These muscles must be flexible enough to allow us to laterally lift or 'abduct' the legs at the hip joint when executing kicks such as roundhouse, side and hook kicks. Similarly, the hamstring group comprises three muscles: the biceps femoris, semitendinosus and semimembranosus. The hamstring muscles bend or 'flex' the leg at the knee joint, but they also have to be flexible enough to allow us to do the opposite: to straighten our legs, and to be able to lift them directly in front of us without restriction, such as in the execution of front kicks and axe kicks.

Essentially, every kick used in Full Contact Kickboxing requires flexibility either in the adductors, the hamstrings, or both. If you have limitations in the flexibility of these muscle groups that are inhibiting your ability to kick properly, then a specialized flexibility routine for these muscle groups is required.

If you have the ability to perform the full splits as a result of your flexibility work, that is a by-product of the training, not the goal. Do not be discouraged if you cannot perform a full splits position. Several of the best kickers in the sport have remarked that they can't do the splits, but that didn't stop them from becoming World Champion Kickboxers. Remember, your goal with adductor and hamstring stretching is to obtain and maintain enough flexibility to be able to execute your kicks to any target whilst minimizing the risk of injury.

When performing these stretches, you should get to a point of mild discomfort – a 'nice burn' as Bill Wallace termed it – in order to optimize the effect of each stretch. If you feel any amount of discomfort beyond this level, you should reduce the stretch immediately to avoid risk of injury. Be very careful and take your time to progress with the routine described below over time.

Seated split stretch (hands behind legs)

Seated split stretch – hands behind legs.

With your legs straight and your toes pointed upward, begin the routine by taking your legs as far apart as you can without experiencing pain. Place your hands on the floor behind your legs, relaxing into the stretch. Hold for 30 seconds.

Seated split stretch (elbows to floor)

After holding the previous stretch for 30 seconds, you will notice that you're able to increase the range of motion slightly. Using your hands, move yourself forward about an inch, increasing the range of motion between your legs, and place your elbows to the floor in front of you. Hold for 30 seconds.

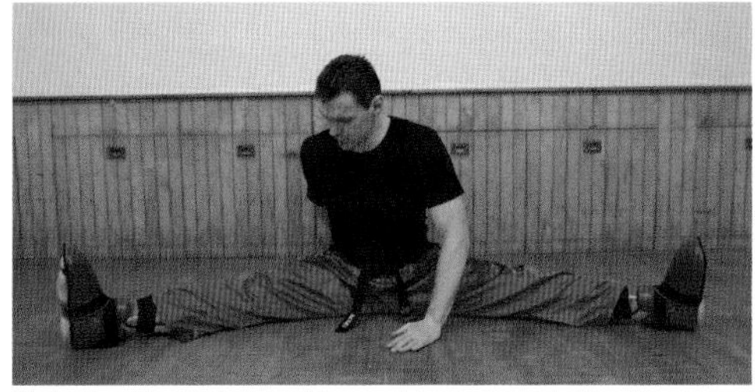

1. Starting position.

2. Push forward.

3. Seated split stretch.

Right hamstring stretch (from seated split stretch)

Reach over to hold your right foot with both hands to stretch the hamstring muscle group of your right leg. Keep both legs straight and hold for 30 seconds.

Right hamstring stretch.

Left hamstring stretch (from seated split stretch)

Reach over to hold your left foot with both hands to stretch the hamstring muscle group of your left leg. Keep both legs straight and hold for 30 seconds.

Left hamstring stretch.

Seated split stretch (elbows to floor)

Place your elbows to the floor directly in front of you, as before. Hold for 30 seconds.

Seated split stretch – elbow to floor.

Pancake stretch

Bring the soles of your feet together as you sit on the floor, hold onto your feet with your hands and gently push your thighs towards the floor with your elbows. Avoid rounding out your back

Pancake stretch.

by bringing your chest up and retaining good posture as you stretch. Hold for 30 seconds.

Right hamstring stretch

Remaining seated, place the bottom of your left foot against the inside of your right thigh and position your upper body so it is directly in-line with your straight right leg (toes up). From this position, reach forward to hold your right foot with both hands to stretch the hamstring muscle group of your right leg. Keep your right leg straight and hold for 30 seconds.

Right hamstring stretch.

Left hamstring stretch

To 'mirror' the right hamstring stretch, place the bottom of your right foot against the inside of your left thigh and position your upper body so it is directly in-line with your straight left leg (toes up). From this position, reach forward to hold your left foot with both hands to stretch the hamstring muscle group of your

Left hamstring stretch.

left leg. Keep your left leg straight and hold for 30 seconds.

If you are able, you can push yourself slightly forward by an inch or so after each of the seated split stretch positions, as was detailed between the first and second seated split stretches. This increases the stretch on the adductors in a gradual, progressive manner as you 'warm into' your stretching programme. However, unless you are already very flexible or advanced in your training, this type of progressive stretching (pushing yourself forward after each stretch) should be limited to a maximum of every other day.

STRETCHING ROUTINES

Stretching is an important part of a complete fitness programme. It is advisable to cool-down and stretch after every workout. Below are three stretching routines: an 8-minute stretch routine with 9 exercises, a more extensive 15-minute stretch routine with 16 exercises and the adductor/hamstring specialized stretch routine. Choose *either* the 8-minute stretch routine or the 15-minute stretch routine after your workout, and complete the adductor/hamstring specialized stretch routine afterwards. Take your time to perform these exercises in the order laid out. Include the 15-minute routine into your training schedule, two to three times per week.

8-minute stretching routine (9 stretches)

Upper back and shoulder stretch
Pull back lat stretch
Chest and biceps stretch
Forearm stretch

Stretching routines.

Piriformis stretch
Kneeling hip flexor stretch
Standing quadriceps stretch
Hamstring stretch
Standing calf/Achilles stretch

15-minute stretching routine (16 stretches)

Neck stretch
Upper back and shoulder stretch
Pull back lat stretch
Chest and shoulder stretch
Triceps stretch
Chest and biceps stretch
Forearm stretch
Core side stretch
Lower back stretch
Piriformis stretch
Kneeling hip flexor stretch
Standing quadriceps stretch
ITB stretch
Hamstring stretch
Standing calf/Achilles stretch
Soleus/Achilles stretch

Keys to Success

- Never bounce when you are stretching. Muscles, tendons and ligaments can be stressed and result in injury.
- Do not force a muscle to overstretch. Once a tension is felt in the muscle, ease off and hold the length where there is not any discomfort.
- A static stretch, when a muscle is lengthened just beyond its natural length and held for more than 30 seconds, is the safest and most effective method of stretching.

Adductor/hamstring specialized stretching routine (8 stretches)

(To be performed *either* after the 8-minute *or* the 15-minute stretching routine)

Seated split stretch (hands behind legs)
Seated split stretch (elbows to floor)
Right hamstring stretch (from seated split stretch)
Left hamstring stretch (from seated split stretch)
Seated split stretch (elbows to floor)
Pancake stretch
Right hamstring stretch
Left hamstring stretch

Stretching is key to success.

Improvements in your flexibility, muscle length, and joint mobility will be noticeable if you stretch on a regular basis. Remember, stretching should not feel painful. If there is pain associated with your stretches, ensure you are executing the movements correctly. If you have any joint problems or issues with your back or neck, consult with your doctor before performing the exercises.

Stretch every day.

TOP TEN
TWINS
TOPTEN

9 SPARRING

Kickboxing requires intense mental focus, a highly developed fitness level, commitment, and passion. The body and mind work in synchrony. Successful Kickboxers clock several thousands of hours of training, executing each movement repeatedly in order to master precise timing and achieve the level of extreme physical conditioning required of this demanding sport.

Sparring introduces a live opponent, taking the defensive nature of the sport to another level. Sparring fine-tunes skills and simulates fight conditions in a controlled environment. Drills practised up to this point will be executed under pressure, providing the ideal opportunity to improve all aspects of performance. As moves are not choreographed, they must be improvised; sparring is therefore more complex and intense than punching the heavy bag or focus mitts.

All defensive and offensive moves must be instinctive and automatic. These skills should be carefully honed on the focus pads. In addition to the requisite physical endurance and skills, it is equally important to have the proper mindset.

Sparring is not for everyone and should be recognized as a potentially dangerous activity; heavy bags do not strike back but sparring partners do. Before engaging in sparring, it is imperative that you are in excellent physical condition. To that end, work on developing the technical skills and physical conditioning over a period of 6 months or longer. When you can endure six or seven rounds on the heavy bag with intensity, run 4 or 5 miles at a 7-minute-mile pace, jump rope for at least 15 to 20 minutes, *and* complete a gruelling

Make intelligent decisions

Know when you are physically able to spar. Understand how you feel when you are experiencing 'good pain' and are able to push through temporary exhaustion. This is what makes you a better Kickboxer. However, respect your body if you are injured, experiencing extreme fatigue or excessive muscle pain. Rest may be necessary in order that minor injuries and symptoms do not become chronic. Always keep your trainer informed, make adjustments to your sparring sessions, and take the time to recover from an injury or illness.

OPPOSITE: Sparring.

session on the focus pads, you *might* be ready to spar.

Only spar under the supervision of an experienced, certified trainer. Follow your trainer's directions. You must wear protective equipment and large sparring gloves (at least 16 ounces). Spar in a boxing ring or on a cushioned surface, not on a hard floor surface.

TYPES OF SPARRING

Directed sparring

With directed sparring, each Kickboxer is given a set of instructions and types of techniques to utilize. Sessions may include one boxer working on defensive moves (deflecting, blocking and slipping), and the other working on offensive moves (throwing punches and kicks). You may do one round of sparring just throwing jabs or a session of throwing punches to the body. The trainer may switch roles and will add more elements into the sparring as the instruction continues. Directed sparring allows the Kickboxer to gain confidence before advancing to free-form sparring.

Directed sparring.

Situational sparring

Situational sparring develops muscle memory and quick reflexes. It helps to familiarize a kickboxer with different fighting styles. As you experience sparring with different opponents and in different situations, you will start to develop your own fighting style.

Free-form sparring

Free-form sparring, also known as 'open' sparring, is the most advanced form of sparring. All aspects of offensive and defensive moves are incorporated into this training and your responses are continually changing. Only spar the number of rounds for which you are able to maintain proper form and technique. Spar shorter rounds until you build your endurance, working your way up to full 2-minute rounds. Increase the number of rounds as your conditioning improves. Spar one to two

Sparring is not fighting!

The goal of a competitive Kickboxing match is to win the contest. Focusing on the quality of your performance, execution, and timing are the goals of sparring. The intensity of a sparring session will be influenced by a number of factors, and it is necessary for Kickboxers to control emotions and tempers. Due to the competitive nature of the sport, if a novice Kickboxer is sparring with a more experienced practitioner, his intensity level may increase due to frustration. By focusing on tactical aspects of the performance during a sparring session, you can learn how to react accordingly in a fight situation instead of retaliating with an emotional response.

more rounds than the number of rounds you would compete, in order to build physical and mental ring conditioning. Incorporate round-robin sparring (sparring one to two rounds with a one-round break in between) into your sessions allowing for training and developing the technical aspects of your performance. Add an additional challenge to your training by decreasing the recovery time by shortening the rest intervals between rounds.

WHAT TO EXPECT THE FIRST TIME YOU SPAR

Depending on your Kickboxing experience, your sparring partner's skill level, and your trainer's knowledge, your first taste of stepping in the ring may be unnerving and will be different from anyone else's. As a novice, your trainer should have you work with an experienced Kickboxer who will not take advantage of your lack of experience. Your trainer will also make sure that you and your sparring partner agree on the pace and intensity of your sparring workout.

New Kickboxers often have difficulty controlling their emotions before a sparring session, due to an increased release of adrenaline in their system; this could lead to a feeling of nervousness or anxiety. Unlike working the heavy bag, where you can move for four or five rounds and punch when you want to, now you have a live opponent chasing you and setting the tempo. A feeling of survival in the ring can create a very different scenario than working on the pads with your trainer. It is difficult to plan under pressure and all the well-practised combinations on the pads and heavy bag may turn into wild swinging punches. Missing your target expends more energy than landing a punch or a kick. You are also concentrating on both throwing and evading techniques at the same time.

Emotions must be kept under control, focusing on the task at hand and being in the moment. Sparring is a training session and there are no winners or losers; if winning becomes a goal, then emotions may influence the result.

Positive visualization

Effective Kickboxers use positive visualization techniques prior to training and during competition. Positive visualization helps to build confidence and improves your ability to perform under pressure and in a variety of situations. Create a mental image of how you want to perform. You may imagine details of a previous best performance, the way it felt and played out. See yourself throwing strong, crisp punches and kicks, moving smoothly around the ring.

Just like warming up or putting on your hand wraps, positive visualization needs to be part of your training ritual.

Sparring gear

Mouth guard

Never spar without a mouthpiece. A good mouthpiece helps prevent cuts inside the mouth, damage to the teeth and supports the jaw. When boxing you want a comfortable fit, as it is important to keep your mouth closed. Gel guards, forming to your teeth, allow for a good fit. Get it in advance because it has to be boiled and formed to your teeth before sparring. The best fit is a dentist-made mouthpiece.

Protective cups

Protect the groin, hips and kidneys from low blows.

Chest protector

The chest region for females is protected from punches.

Shin guards

Your shin guards will be of the same specifications as those used in regulated Full Contact Kickboxing competition (*see* Chapter 2). Ensure they fit snugly without moving around while you kick, but are not so tight as to cause discomfort in the calves; this could limit your ring movement and your ability to flex your feet at the ankles properly.

Kick boots

Like your shin guards, your kicks boots will be of the same specifications as those you would use in regulated competition (*see* Chapter 2). Because the kick boot is designed for use in the ring or on the mat, it covers the top of the foot (instep), the ankle and the back of the heel. The bottoms of your feet are exposed when you're wearing kick boots. For everyday training such as shadowboxing and bag work, if the floor is not cushioned or matted, wear a cross trainer shoe. Save the bottoms of your feet from picking up potential scratches or infections that could halt your training. Keep your kick boots for the ring.

Protective head gear

The best head gear models offer extra protection without compromising your vision. Make sure the head gear fits snugly, not sliding around or obstructing your vision. If your head gear comes with adjustable straps, ensure that the loop-and-fasten instructions are correctly followed in order to avoid the aforementioned issues.

Hand wraps

Even if you are wearing the best boxing gloves available, you always need to ensure your hands are wrapped effectively for protection. In order to have the best protection for your hands, effective hand wrapping is essential.

Sparring gloves

These 'oversized' boxing gloves are made with extra shock absorbing foam and are 16 ounces in size, since you will be striking an opponent and not a heavy bag. They are available in either a lace-up or Velcro-fastened version. Make sure the gloves are in good condition with no tears or cracks in the leather and check inside the gloves to ensure that the foam and protective padding is not breaking up. Only use these gloves for sparring, not bag work or focus pad work.

DEFENSIVE MOVES

The number one rule in combat sports is, 'Protect yourself at all times!' There is a constant shift between offensive and defensive movement when sparring. Before launching an offensive attack, you must first learn to protect yourself.

Keep your hands up

The arms and gloves act as a basic shield to defend the body and head. The arms are kept close to the sides of the body by the ribs, protecting the rib cage and solar plexus, and the fist/gloves up by the face and chin to protect the head (*see* Chapter 2).

Hands up.

Head movement.

Blocking.

Head movement

Constant head movement can disrupt your opponent's rhythm and allows you to slip your opponent's punches. This leaves your hands free to counter-punch. Always keep your hands up in the protective position and do not make the mistake of dropping your hands when moving your head. Where the head goes, the hands follow.

Watch fight footage of Massimo Brizi to see how his upper body movement, head fakes and unpredictability startles his opponents and renders them unable to concentrate on their own offence.

Blocking

The most fundamental defensive method is blocking. With your hands up and tight against your head, use the outside portion of the gloves to block headshots. Keep the elbows close to the body and use the elbow or forearm to block body punches. From this platform, you are in prime position to slip, weave and counter-punch.

Curtis Bush was an expert at blocking punches and kicks. As the techniques made contact with his gloves and arms, he would turn slightly with the direction of the technique and 'roll' with the impact. This is referred to as 'rolling with the punches' (*see* Chapter 3).

With time and experience, you develop the ability to instantaneously react accordingly, whether that's to block and roll with a technique, to 'stiff-arm' block it and absorb the impact on your guard, or to go to another defensive manoeuvre such as a parry, a slip, or a bob and weave.

Parrying

Parrying a punch involves 'catching' it and then redirecting it aside. The body does not move, only the hand. To parry, turn the palm of your glove to catch the knuckles of the opponent's glove. Keep your glove at your chin and wait for the punch to come to you. Do not reach or paw for the punch. Protect yourself by keeping your arms and elbows close to the torso (*see* Chapter 3).

Dan parries James' jab.

Dan weaves under James' hook.

Parrying works best against straight punches. Parry with the right hand against the opponent's left hand. This leaves your left hand free to counter-punch instantaneously. Likewise, your left hand defends against your opponent's incoming right, giving an opportunity for a counter-punch. This rule applies whether you are in an orthodox or southpaw stance: parry the right hand with your left hand, and the left hand with your right hand.

Once you are confident with parrying, you can manipulate it by deflecting and redirecting your opponent's glove down, either to the inside or outside. Timing the parry is crucial as you leave yourself open when you do not redirect the oncoming punch at the right moment. You can use parries to defend against uppercuts. Use the opposite hand to parry the incoming uppercut. This is a risky move, and it is better to avoid the uppercut by blocking it with your forearm, or stepping back and counter-punching. In their prime, John Longstreet and James Warring were great at parrying punches.

Bobbing and weaving

Bobbing and weaving refers to moving the head and body beneath an incoming punch. It is a great defensive technique against hooking punches and can be used against straight punches too, such as if you slip your opponent's jab, and then weave under their follow-up cross.

Move the head underneath the incoming punch, bending at your knees quickly and keeping your eyes on your opponent. As you duck down, shift your body weight slightly to the left or right, 'weaving' your head and shoulders underneath the punch. Against a left hook, weave to your right. Against a right hook, weave to your left. Once you have dodged the punch, return quickly to your boxing stance. Bobbing and weaving requires excellent timing. It works well against sluggers that like to throw big looping hooks. To become comfortable and effective with bobbing and weaving, work with your coach using focus pad drills.

A Kickboxer who was a master at this technique was the late, great Demetrius 'The Greek' Havanas. Standing at 5 feet, 5 inches tall, Havanas would weave his way under a variety of techniques from his usually-taller opponents as he advanced towards them to unleash a barrage of punches and kicks.

Slipping

Slipping is an effective defensive technique and gets you out of the way of an oncoming punch and at the same time keeps you in the range to counter-punch. Slipping can be used instead of blocking the oncoming punch,

James slips Dan's cross.

utilizing a side-to-side movement of the head and shoulders and bending the knees so that the oncoming punch 'slips' safely past you. The body stays directly over the legs, slightly forward and not leaning back.

Slipping an oncoming punch is an art, and can put your opponent at a disadvantage. It effectively frees up your arms to counter-punch. Choosing the right moment to slip is critical. The timing and confidence to utilize this advanced defensive move needs to be practised during shadowboxing, target mitt drills and controlled sparring. Excessive slipping wastes energy.

Examples of fighters who exhibit excellent slipping skills include Don Wilson, Curtis Bush, Rick Roufus and Massimo Brizi. These Kickboxing legends would slip *as* they punched, moving their head off the line of their opponent's punch whilst intercepting the attack with a punch of their own. This technique is extremely effective and can cause an instant knockdown or knockout.

Slipping the jab

Hands up, knees bent. Move your head and shoulders to the outside of the jab – just enough to clear it. Counter-punch options include slipping and counter-punching with a jab to the head or body; alternatively, after slipping a jab, counter with a rear hand punch to the head or body.

Slipping the cross

With your hands up, bend your knees slightly, slip outside of the cross. Counter-punch option: return with a lead hook to the body or lead hook the head.

Slip a jab.

Slip a cross.

Slipping tips

- The whole point of slipping is to avoid a punch and create an opening for a counter-punch.
- Slipping keeps your arms free so you can counter-punch.
- If you have avoided a punch by slipping, that is a good thing, but you do not want to continually use slipping just to avoid punches. It is a waste of energy and opportunity.
- If you are not going to counter-punch, then you are better off blocking or parrying the punch.
- If you continually slip without responding with a counter-punch, your opponent will recognize that you are not going to throw a punch, learn your slipping pattern and retaliate.

Successful Kickboxers use defensive moves to avoid punches and at the same time set up their own attacks. When you block, slip, or parry a punch, come out of that defensive move with a counter-punch. The more you spar the more you will become aware of your opponent's counter-punches. For example, when you throw a jab, you may expect a right cross from your opponent. Work on target mitt counter-punch drills with your coach to develop natural defensive reflexes.

> **Keys to Success**
>
> **FUNDAMENTAL DEFENSIVE TIPS**
>
> - Never take your eyes off your opponent.
> - Keep your hands up and chin down.
> - Keep moving.
> - Get back on balance quickly.
> - Do not lean back to avoid punches.
> - Stay out of the corners.
> - Stay off ropes.
> - Move your head or your opponent will move it for you.

OFFENSIVE MOVES

Movement

Effective movement is an offensive tool as well as an essential defensive method. Fluid movement is essential in the ring, and it's important for movement to be well practised in the gym.

Range

Range is the amount of distance between you and your opponent. The use of effective range will allow you to hit your opponent while giving you the time to manoeuvre defensively.

Jab, jab, jab!

As the most frequently thrown punch, the main purpose of the jab is to keep your opponent off guard and at a safe distance. It sets up your entire repertoire of punches and kicks, keeps your opponent off balance and can be used to dictate the pace of the fight. The jab is the fastest and safest punch in your arsenal. Start off your offence with crisp, clean jabs.

Clean techniques

Your kicks and punches must land above the belt of the opponent and in front or at the sides of the head or body. A 'slapping punch' or making contact with the palm side of the glove is a common mistake. Strikes with any part of the arm other than the glove are illegal, as are blows to the back of the head and the kidneys.

Combinations

Do not get comfortable with throwing just jabs and lead leg side kicks. If you can catch your opponent with your jab, it is time to add combinations and keep him off-guard. Start to throw one-twos (jab-cross) and put more power into your punches. Sometimes you can pierce your opponent's defence on the first kick or punch thrown, and sometimes it opens up on the second or third technique. Keep throwing combinations to take advantage of all opportunities. Stay busy.

Feints

'Feints' or 'fakes' create opportunities to disrupt your opponent's rhythm. By drawing your opponent into responding to the feint, you are able to produce an opportunity for a counter technique. The incomplete attacks of feinting, such as slightly moving your shoulders, fists, feet or body will cause a reaction from your opponent. For example, feint a jab to the body, so your opponent will drop their guard, and quickly throw a jab to the head. Feint with your feet: feint a lead leg roundhouse kick to the body, then without putting your foot down, quickly snap it up to the face. Use your movement around the ring to deceive your opponent. Quickly move your feet a half step to the left and then move the feet to the right, possibly creating an opening and an opportunity (*see* Chapter 2).

Counter techniques

Countering is the most important offensive skill to learn. You have a very small opportunity to respond with a counter-punch or kick while your opponent is trying to score on you. You have to think about both protecting yourself and at the same time landing your own effective technique. With practice, more creative counters can be learned.

- The best time to hit your opponent is when he is throwing a punch or a kick.
- Counter techniques stop your opponent's momentum.
- Counter techniques will make your opponent cautious.
- The only way to go from defence to offence is to counter your opponent's moves.

Examples of possible counter-punches

These combinations apply when you and your opponent or sparring partner are in 'matching' stances, i.e., both Kickboxers are in an orthodox stance, or they're both in a southpaw stance.

When your opponent throws a jab

- Parry with your rear glove and throw a counter-jab straight back into the head. Keep the jab shoulder high and chin tucked to protect from a one-two (jab-cross) retaliation.
- Slip to the outside and then throw a jab to the head or the body.
- Duck, bend your knees, lowering your body and throw a counter-jab straight to your opponent's solar plexus.
- Duck and jab and throw a cross to the body.

When your opponent throws a jab to the body

- Block the punch with the lead elbow and come back with a cross to the head.
- Take a half-step back to avoid the punch and quickly move forward with a quick hook to the head.

When your opponent throws a cross

- Block with your lead glove as you roll with the punch. Immediately come back with your own cross.
- Catch/parry the incoming cross with your lead glove. Throw a quick cross to the head.
- Slip to the outside and throw a lead hook to the body.

- Slip to the outside and throw a cross to the head or body.

When your opponent throws a cross to the body

- Block with the elbow and throw a cross to the head.
- Take a half step back. Quickly move forward and throw a lead uppercut to the head.

When your opponent throws a hook

- Block the punch and come back with a straight one-two combination.
- Weave under the hook and come back with a hook-cross combination to the body.
- Take a half step back to avoid the hook. Come back with a straight counter-punch and then a quick jab to the head.

When your opponent throws a hook to the body

- Block the punch with your elbow. With your free hand, counter with a hook to the head or the body.
- Take a half step back and throw a jab to the head.

When your opponent throws an uppercut

- If your opponent telegraphs (winds-up) the uppercut, throw a quick jab, or one-two to the head.
- Catch the uppercut and throw a quick uppercut to the head.

Remember to move your head and body after throwing combinations. Constantly give your opponent angles. Never stand in front of them for too long, allowing them to get set. Practise counter-punching drills at three-quarter speed with a partner. These sessions should always be supervised with a coach.

Examples of countering kicks

When your opponent throws a front kick

Retaining your on-guard position, block your opponent's front kick with your lead forearm and turn your upper body slightly to 'roll' with the kick. This causes your opponent to momentarily fall off balance. As your opponent's kicking leg 'falls' back down to the floor, quickly throw a one-two (jab-cross) combination to the chin.

This technique works well whether the opponent throws a lead or rear front kick, but regardless of which stance they're in, it works particularly well if your opponent's kicking leg corresponds to your lead arm (i.e. a southpaw lead right arm defending a right front kick). This is because as you turn your body, you move your opponent's kicking leg outward, exposing their centre line and enabling you to land your punches while they're 'squared up'. This technique can also be effective against the lead leg side kick.

When your opponent throws a roundhouse kick

Many fighters, even professional fighters, don't protect themselves adequately when they throw front and roundhouse kicks. Because of this, it is wise to counter your opponent's roundhouse kicks whenever possible. A great counter to roundhouse kicks to the head is to defend the kick with your corresponding-side arm/glove and quickly counter with a cross.

Examples of intercepting kicks

If you can beat your opponent to the punch, and in these cases, to the kick, then you will be able to cause significant damage as you and your opponent collide, each with forward momentum. The momentum of your punch or kick into the momentum of your opponent's head or body can easily cause a knockdown or knockout.

In fighting stance.

Block...

... and roll with the kick...

... follow up jab...

... and a cross.

In fighting stance.

Block the roundhouse.

Counter with a cross.

At range.

Block the roundhouse.

Counter with a cross.

Intercepting techniques can be extremely effective in causing significant damage and in disrupting your opponent's rhythm. Don't try to intercept every single technique your opponent throws. There are times to defend, to defend and counter, and to simply move away from an attack rather than trying to intercept it. There must be an element of unpredictability in your tactics.

Intercepting a roundhouse kick with your jab

As your opponent attempts a roundhouse kick, push off your back foot and advance

In fighting stance...

as you land a stiff jab to the head. If timed correctly, this technique is effective whether your opponent throws a lead or rear roundhouse kick.

Intercepting a roundhouse kick with your cross

As your opponent attempts a roundhouse kick, push off your back foot and advance as you land a cross to the head. As with the jab, using the cross to intercept an opponent's roundhouse kick can be effective whichever leg they attempt to kick with.

... step in with a jab...

... to intercept the kick.

From range...

... step in with a cross...

... to intercept the kick.

Side kick.

1. In fighting stance.

2. James drops to the floor as he sees...

Intercepting a roundhouse kick with a side kick

As your opponent attempts a roundhouse kick, push off your back foot and advance as you land a side kick to the body. As with the punches, using the side kick to intercept an opponent's roundhouse kick can be effective whichever leg they attempt to kick with.

Intercepting a roundhouse kick with a sweep

As your opponent initiates a roundhouse kick, drop to the floor with the outside of your lead leg making contact with the floor. Brace yourself with your lead arm against the floor as you simultaneously sweep with your rear leg. This

3. ... Dan initiate a rear leg roundhouse kick.

4. James sweeps Dan's support leg as Dan kicks...

5. ... sending him to the floor on his back.

technique requires excellent timing and you must commit to the manoeuvre once you begin the drop. Keep your chin down, your rear shoulder high and rear arm in front of your face to defend against any stray techniques from your opponent, in case their roundhouse kick was actually a fake-technique to set something else up.

Countering your opponent's sweeps

If your lead leg is swept out from under you, but you're still standing, you won't have the balance or leverage to be able to throw a powerful punch as an instantaneous counter-attack. However, you can score with lead leg kicking techniques such as side kicks and hook kicks, particularly if your lead leg was swept from the outside of your lead foot.

Countering a sweep with a side kick

As your opponent's sweep lands, rather than allowing it to knock you off balance, 'go with' the force of the sweep and chamber your knee

1. In fighting stance.

2. Dan uses a sweep to James' front foot.

3. James uses the momentum of the sweep to chamber his leg...

4. ... and counters with a side kick to the body.

2. Dan uses a sweep to James' front foot.

into your body, enabling you to launch a hard side kick to the mid-section.

Countering a sweep with a hook kick

As in the case of the side kick-counter, as you feel your lead foot being swept out of the on-guard position, chamber your knee and launch a hook kick to the side of your opponent's head.

3. James uses the momentum of the sweep to chamber his leg...

1. In fighting stance.

4. ... and counters with a hook kick to the head.

KEYS TO SUCCESS

FUNDAMENTAL OFFENSIVE TIPS

- Move and jab.
- Establish your lead weapons: your jab and your lead leg kicking techniques.
- Don't hesitate with your counter techniques.
- Counter-punch in combinations.
- Do not be predictable.
- Mix up your combinations: throw punches and kicks with both hands and feet.
- Feint punches and kicks.
- Throw punches to the body.
- Work harder than your opponent.

DIFFERENT STYLES OF KICKBOXING

Take every opportunity to spar with different opponents. Kickboxing against a variety of styles will give you a better understanding of how to fight your opponents. Stay focused even when you get hit. Shake it off. Successful Kickboxers maintain focus even when they get hit.

Sparring with a taller fighter

A taller opponent has a reach advantage and will be expecting you to try to get inside to land your punches. Never underestimate your opponent, whatever their size, apparent speed or strength.

- Be busier; use your kicks and throw two- and three-punch combinations to get inside.
- Work the body once you get inside, making your opponent drop his arms to protect his body and creating an opportunity for head punches.
- Utilize slipping and moving from side to side, making your opponent look for you.
- Move to your opponent's jab side, away from the strong straight punches and rear leg roundhouse kicks.
- Throw in feints, mix up your techniques and be unpredictable.

Sparring with a shorter fighter

When you spar against a shorter opponent they will have to try to get inside to work the body, throwing shorter punches and will duck under your punches. This will take away your reach advantage.

- Work your lead leg: side kicks, round kicks and hook kicks. Jab and keep your distance, preventing your opponent from getting inside.
- Follow your jab with strong punch combinations and roundhouse kicks with both legs.
- Snap your techniques, keeping your opponent on the end of your punches and kicks.
- Be active, move around using the entire ring, making your opponent move and expend energy.
- Keep your chin tucked in.

Sparring with a wild Kickboxer

Wild boxers are often inexperienced and scared. Their techniques are unpredictable and you do not want to get caught with a lucky punch or kick.

- Stay true to your style of fighting and your game plan.
- Maintain proper form, so you do not leave yourself open to lucky shots.
- Be ready for the wild boxer to take lunging steps as they move forward. Side step, bob and weave, step backward, to keep them off-guard.

- Wild boxers tend to throw looping, wide punches. Take advantage of this and throw straight punches down the middle.
- Mix your techniques up with feints.
- Move them backward with numerous jabs and side kicks, as often they are not comfortable fighting when they are moving backward.

Sparring with a slugger

Sluggers have a hard, forceful punch and tend to move straight forward to attack their opponent. They often will take two to three shots in order to set up and land their own big punches. Demetrius 'Oaktree' Edwards is one of the best examples of this type of fighter. The World Title battle between Demetrius Edwards and the late, great Steve Shepherd – a Heavyweight versus a Middleweight – demonstrates the classic slugger versus slick fighter match-up. Shepherd won the bout by employing these tactics:

- Constantly move, creating lots of angles, so the slugger has less time to get set.
- Move quickly in and out, attacking suddenly and throwing rapid-fire jabs.
- Do not stand toe-to-toe. Stay out of their reach.
- Circle away from the slugger's power side.
- Throw feints to gauge the reaction of your opponent.

Sparring with a 'slick' fighter

'Slick' fighters have great footwork and like to move a lot. They have a wide range of kicks and punches at their disposal, utilizing a variety of angles and defensive tactics.

- Be ready to counter-punch. 'Slick' fighters tend to throw multiple jabs, so be prepared to counter-punch.
- Use lots of head movement to off-set their jab.
- Mix up how you react to their jab. Parry the jab, slip the jab, or move away.
- Stay in control. 'Slick' fighters wait for you to make a mistake. Be patient, use your jab and your lead leg to create openings and then throw effective combinations.
- Force the action, moving your opponent backward.

Sparring with a fighter in an opposite stance

Depending on your dominant hand, or your individual preference, you will fight out of either an orthodox or southpaw stance (*see* Chapter 2).

It's not uncommon in Kickboxing to find yourself sparring with or fighting against someone in an opposite stance to you. If you're orthodox, the majority of your sparring and competition is likely to be against other orthodox Kickboxers, with some southpaw sparring partners and opponents being presented to you less frequently. If you are a southpaw, you are likely to find more orthodox sparring partners and opponents than fellow southpaws.

Southpaw is the 'normal' stance for a left-handed Kickboxer. This boxer has his right hand and right foot forward. They lead with right jabs and follow with left crosses and right hooks. Because most Kickboxers fight in the orthodox style (right-handed fighter with the left lead), it can be challenging for them when sparring against a southpaw (left-handed fighter with the right lead). Because southpaws have more opportunities to spar with orthodox fighters, the southpaw has a greater advantage.

- When an opponent from the opposite stance throws a jab, parry with your lead hand. Counter with a cross to the head or body.
- Lead with crosses. While you should still use your jab judiciously, you can lead with crosses and expect to score more frequently against an opponent in the opposite stance.

- Circle to the *outside* of their lead foot, away from their cross – if you're orthodox, circle left; if you're southpaw, circle right.
- Feint with a cross and follow with a lead hand hook.

Keys to Success

Error:	Signalling your intentions (telegraphing). The fist is pulled back or drops slightly before executing the punch.
Quick fix:	Fire crisp clean punches directly from your chin to the target.
Error:	Fighter drops one hand while throwing the other.
Quick fix:	Dropping your non-punching hand from the on-guard/protective position leaves you vulnerable to counter-punches. Practise in front of a mirror. During focus pad training, your coach can tap you with the pad when you drop your hand as a reminder.
Error:	Not throwing enough. New Kickboxers often become frustrated if their kicks and punches are not landing. There is a tendency to stop throwing punches, especially if they are getting hit.
Quick fix:	You have to throw a punch in order to land a punch. Be aggressive. Combinations create openings.
Error:	Becoming frustrated or angry.
Quick fix:	There is no place for frustration or anger in sparring. Successful Kickboxers must maintain control at all times. If you cannot handle getting hit or you get upset that your techniques are not effective, then you are not emotionally ready to spar.
Error:	Poor conditioning.
Quick fix:	Ensure you have the proper physical conditioning to spar. Do not waste your time, your sparring partner's time and your coach's time. Be honest with yourself. Dedicate yourself to your running and gym training before you step into the ring to spar. Train hard, so your performance in the ring can be explosive and intense for the entire training session.
Error:	Hesitating with your techniques.
Quick fix:	A half-thrown punch is worthless. It is a waste of energy and leaves you vulnerable to counter-punches. Commit to your techniques and throw them with confidence.
Error:	Getting trapped in the corner.
Quick fix:	If your opponent has backed you into a corner, disrupt his attack with quick punches to create an opening. When an opening presents itself, rapidly move to get out of the corner. Your defensive options are limited when caught in a corner. You can fake-step one way, and then quickly move in the other direction to get out of the corner.
Error:	Flinching, not keeping your eyes open and/or panicking and holding your breath when punches come your way.
Quick fix:	One way of breaking the habit of flinching is to practise the 'tapping drill' with your coach or partner. Move forward and backward, with your hands held high in the guard position, as light punches are thrown at your gloves in a random manner. Get used to blocking punches, developing a comfortable breathing rhythm and keeping your eyes open.

Set specific goals for each training session. Prepare yourself by using positive visualization. Be in the best physical shape possible in order to practise your skills and give maximum attention and effort. Effective controlled sparring develops reaction time, improves conditioning, and improves your ring generalship.

10 TRAINING ROUTINES AND WORKOUTS

As important as any facet of Kickboxing training is the structure of your training schedule. The layout of your runs, workouts and supplementary exercises such as weight training and flexibility work throughout each week is of paramount importance if you want to get the most out of your training. Additionally, your training schedule needs to be tailored to you. Of course, you need to be committed to your training and you need to make time for your sessions. But within that construct, your work and other life commitments must be taken into consideration when planning your training schedule. There is no point in designing a high-frequency, high-volume and complicated training programme if you have no realistic way of following it. Start by organizing your overall daily schedule and then design your workouts to accommodate that schedule.

Your training will vary depending on your goals at any given time. For example, if you are between fights and don't currently have a fight scheduled, your workouts should keep you within reaching distance of the condition you'd expect to be in for a professional fight, but not be so long and arduous as to lead to overtraining, fatigue and potential for injuries and illness. Training for a fight requires you to push yourself to peak condition, but to do so in a smart and effective way so as to avoid the aforementioned pitfalls: overtraining, illness and injury. Training for a fight should be challenging enough that you wouldn't be able to follow such a schedule indefinitely; your schedule would need to be eased after so many weeks or you would risk these pitfalls. That's why there is a difference between training when you don't have a fight scheduled, and training for a fight (i.e. training to be at your absolute best on a given night).

THE WORKOUTS

Two workouts are detailed in this chapter. The first is the Maintenance Workout, designed for those periods when you don't have a fight scheduled, but you are still training in anticipation of your next bout being organized. Skill and fitness developments are still achieved over the long term when a fighter is consistent with maintenance workouts. This programme is to be followed five or six days a week.

The Champ's Workout Programme cranks up the elements of the Maintenance Workout

OPPOSITE: Axe kick.

to the maximum and is designed to prepare you for professional bouts. This is a 6- to 8-week workout programme, 6 days a week.

The Maintenance Workout (5–6 days/week)

Perform the Maintenance Workout five or six days per week. You should be running 4–5 miles in the mornings before you perform your Kickboxing workout later in the day (*see* Chapter 6). Additionally, you should be going through the weight training regimen three days per week (*see* Chapter 7). The Maintenance Workout includes heavy bag, jumping rope, shadowboxing and focus pad training. The minimal pieces of equipment required are boxing gloves, kick boots, shin guards, a heavy bag, and a jump rope.

Shadowboxing warm-up (1 × 2-minute round)

Shadowboxing warms up your working muscles and prepares you mentally to work on the different bags and on focus pads. It also re-orientates you to the proper execution of the punches and kicks. Ensure there is adequate space to move around and execute your techniques. If a mirror is available, visually check to make sure your hands are held high, your body position is in the proper stance, and your punches and kicks are crisp and clean. Always return the hands back to protect your chin. Add movement with your feet, head, and body, keeping balanced and executing your techniques smoothly.

During the 1-minute rest, stretch out any muscles that feel tight. Refer to Chapter 8 for specific exercises. Loosen up the shoulders, hip flexors, and legs.

Shadowboxing (3 × 2-minute rounds)

Throw your punches and kicks with more intensity. Move around and mix up the techniques, moving forward and backward, and side-to-side. Develop smooth transitions for your punches, your kicks and your footwork. Balance is the key and weight transfer should be effortless. Concentrate on fundamental techniques: the punches, front kicks, roundhouse kicks, side kicks and hook kicks. Focus on your technique until it becomes second nature. Get used to working for a full 2 minutes. Stay relaxed but throw your techniques with speed, power and defensive awareness.

Jump rope (4 × 2-minute rounds)

Start by jumping at a moderate pace, keeping the footwork basic. As you become more experienced, increase your jumping intensity. This can be accomplished by moving at a faster pace or by performing more intricate footwork, such as scissors, jumping jacks and even adding some sprints (*see* Chapter 5). The goal is to jump for 2 minutes straight, take a 1-minute break, and then repeat jumping two more times with a 1-minute break. This 1-minute break gives you time to stretch out tight calf muscles and reduce your breathing rate. Remember if you are having difficulty with continuous jumping or with executing the footwork, go back to the neutral move by placing both handles in one hand and rotate the rope at the side of your body. The goal of jumping rope is to condition your cardiovascular system, so you want to keep your breathing rate elevated.

Heavy bag (6 × 2-minute rounds)

Hit the bag for 2 minutes, and then take a 1-minute rest. Complete five rounds total. Start in the classic Kickboxing stance with your hands up and throw jabs as you move around the bag. Your jab is your range finder, so start by throwing plenty of jabs to establish an effective distance from the bag and set a good pace. Keep busy, ensuring your movement and combinations flow easily and there are no long pauses between punches. Start throwing 'one-twos' (a jab followed by a cross) and add front, round and side kicks to the fray. Visualize an opponent in front of you and keep moving.

Simulate a body attack by bending the legs and lowering your body, punching the mid-section of the bag. Find your rhythm and move naturally with the swinging motion of the bag. Find a consistent pace that you can continue with and persevere to the end of the round. For the second and third rounds, work on three and four punch-kick combinations (*see* Chapter 3). Keep moving during your 1-minute rest, walking around the bag, reducing the heart rate slightly and planning your next round.

Focus pads (3 × 2-minute rounds)

When training on the focus pads, concentrate on the proper execution of your strikes and balanced footwork. Keep the combinations basic. Establish a pattern of throwing many crisp jabs, continually moving in between the throws. The catcher controls the action and sets the workout pace, calling out the combinations and keeping the striker in view at all times. The striker must remember to listen for the commands from the catcher, execute the techniques and then move away, ready for the next command. As you become more comfortable throwing and catching kicks and punches, increase the speed and work on more complicated combinations (*see* Chapter 4).

No-partner option

If you do not have partner, you can use the heavy bag as an alternative workout option.

Heavy bag ladder drill

This drill challenges your straight punching technique, foot movement, upper body conditioning and endurance. Try to complete this drill within 6 minutes.

Ladder 1: throw twelve jabs. Reduce the number of jabs you throw by one each time, continuing down the ladder until you throw just one jab.

Take a 1-minute rest.

Ladder 2: throw twelve one-two punch combinations (jab-cross). Reduce the number by one each time continuing down the ladder until you throw just one, one-two punch combination.

Shadowboxing cool down (1 × 2-minute round)

Throw a variety of techniques at 50–60 per cent effort. Even though you are not throwing as hard as you did during your workout, it is still important to focus on the proper form and technical execution. Keep your feet moving side-to-side and front and back. Allow your heart rate to lower and catch your breath.

Stretch

Select stretches for all the main muscle groups you have trained. Hold each stretch for 30–60 seconds (*see* Chapter 8).

Running: on each of your training days, you should be running 4–5 miles (*see* Chapter 6) in the morning before you go to the gym later in the day.

Weight training: complete all exercises in the prescribed routine (*see* Chapter 7) on Mondays, Wednesdays and Fridays *before* your Kickboxing workouts.

The Champ's Workout Programme (6 days/week for 6–8 weeks)

For the Champ's Workout, the training is increased to the maximum to prepare to fight. This training programme is designed for nine-round professional contests, and a focused commitment is required to carry this programme out. Decide with your coach whether to follow a five-day or six-day per week schedule for best results. Always monitor your body for signs of overtraining. If you have nine weeks' notice before your fight, a good strategy would be to train five days per week for the first four weeks, and six days per week for the second four weeks. During the last week before the fight, your training should be gradually

THE MAINTENANCE WORKOUT (5–6 DAYS/WEEK)

Shadowboxing warm-up (1 × 2-minute round)	Shadowbox, working on the basic punches and kicks. Focus on proper technique.
Shadowboxing (3 × 2-minute rounds)	Add more movement while throwing more combinations. Add real intent to your punches and kicks (*see* Chapter 2).
Jump rope (4 × 2-minute rounds)	Jump for 2 minutes straight, take a 1-minute break and repeat jumping for three more rounds with a 1-minute break in between (*see* Chapter 5).
Heavy bag (6 × 2-minute rounds)	Hit the bag for 2 minutes, and then take a 1-minute rest. Complete six rounds total. Ensure your movement is balanced and your Kickboxing combinations flow in a smooth manner (*see* Chapter 4).
Partner drill: focus pads (3 × 2-minute rounds)	Complete three rounds on the focus pads, throwing a variety of punch-kick combinations (*see* Chapter 4).
No-partner option: heavy bag ladder drill (6 minutes)	Ladder 1: throw twelve jabs, reducing down to one jab. Take a 1-minute rest. Ladder 2: throw twelve one-two punch combinations, reducing down to one-two punch combination.
Shadowboxing to cool down (1 × 2-minute round)	End with shadowboxing, punching with light intent. Reduce your heart rate.
Stretch	Allow time to properly stretch out all the muscle groups and joint areas (*see* Chapter 8).

reduced to a minimal amount before taking two full days of rest before the fight.

Run 4–6 miles in the mornings before you perform your Kickboxing workout later in the day (*see* Chapter 6). Additionally, three days per week, you should be going through the weight training regimen *before* your Kickboxing training (*see* Chapter 7).

Shadowboxing warm-up (1 × 2-minute round)

Throw light punches and kicks to start, focusing on proper execution. Begin with straight punches and then add hooks and uppercuts. Continue moving for 2 minutes.

Shadowboxing (3 × 2-minute rounds)

Now that you have warmed up, put intensity behind your punches and kicks, throwing your techniques at full speed and power. Move and throw at your 'virtual opponent'. Practise offensive and defensive moves.

Jump rope (continuous for 15 minutes)

For your jump rope training session, start by jumping at a moderate pace for the first few minutes to set your jumping rhythm. Challenge yourself by adding a variety of footwork and rope moves. Perform double unders, cross-overs and speed sprints within your training (*see* Chapter 5).

Sparring (Monday, Wednesday and Friday: 6–10 × 2-minute rounds)

If you have a partner, complete between eight and twelve rounds of sparring. Always wear all of your equipment when sparring: 16oz boxing gloves, headgear, a mouthpiece, and your kick boots, shin guards and groin protector. When training for an eight to twelve round fight, your other training protocols have also increased in their volume and/or duration. Sparring between eight and twelve rounds is enough for a fight with the rounds in the same range. Sparring twelve rounds for an eight-round fight can be of great benefit to getting into your best form. But be careful not to overdo it. Closely monitor your body, and if you and your coach deem that a nine-round sparring session is sufficient for a nine-round fight, then stick to that. Obviously, the training for such a fight is arduous and will require discipline and persistence, even on days when you're tired. There's a difference between being sensible and lazy, so be honest with yourself and train to your best *without* ending up overtrained or injured. You should know your body by the time you get to this level.

Heavy bag (6–10 × 2-minute rounds)

Train on the heavy bag as though you are facing an actual opponent in the ring, constantly moving while throwing combinations. Include feints, slips, and weaving moves into the mix and visualize deceiving your opponent in order to set up offensive opportunities (*see* Chapter 3). Adding these subtle movements adds another element to your heavy bag training. Coordinate your footwork and strikes with the swinging motion of the bag. Remember real Kickboxing matches do not have long periods of inactivity. Throw plenty of techniques and keep moving to simulate real fight situations. Move around during the 1-minute rest period and plan your next round. (If you've already sparred, you can perform six rounds on the heavy bag instead of ten, if preferred.)

Focus pads (6 × 2-minute rounds)

Focus pad training allows you to bring all of your Kickboxing skills into play. This dynamic training sharpens your offensive and defensive moves, reflexes, balance, and develops total body strength and endurance. When in serious training, you want to throw a wide variety of punch-kick combinations and at a high level of intensity. If you are proficient at executing the advanced combinations described in Chapter 4, you may want to develop your own combinations. When creating your own combinations, ensure a logical sequence is followed and that each punch smoothly sets up the next punch, kick, or movement.

No-partner option

If you do not have partner, you can use the heavy bag as an alternative workout option.

Heavy bag ladder drill

This drill challenges your straight punching technique, foot movement, upper body conditioning and endurance. Try to complete this drill within 6 minutes.

Ladder 1: throw twelve jabs. Reduce the number of jabs you throw by one each time, continuing down the ladder until you throw just one jab.

Take a 1-minute rest.

Ladder 2: throw twelve one-two punch combinations (jab-cross). Reduce the number by one each time, continuing down the ladder until you throw just a single one-two punch combination.

Double-end bag (3 × 2-minute rounds)

Throw punch combinations and slips ensuring you are in a balanced position reacting to the quick movement and the rebound action of the double-end bag. Develop your timing and rhythm, constantly moving and throwing rapid-fire punches (*see* Chapter 3). Rest for 1 minute in between rounds and before hitting the speed bag.

Speed bag (6–8 minutes)

Challenge your upper body endurance by hitting the speed bag at a fast pace for 6–8 minutes. Rest for 1 minute before moving onto the shadowboxing.

Shadowboxing (3 × 2-minute rounds)

Focus on proper technique as you move and throw punches and kicks during another three rounds of shadowboxing. Most fighters don't finish their workout in this fashion as it is very difficult after all the training beforehand. 'Great'

Scott Ashley always finished his workouts in this way as he knew he would gain extra benefit.

Stretch

Perform stretching exercises, holding each stretch for 30 to 60 seconds (*see* Chapter 8).

Running: on each of your training days, you should be running 4–6 miles (*see* Chapter 6) in the morning before you go to the gym later in the day.

Weight training: complete all exercises in the prescribed routine (*see* Chapter 7) on Mondays, Wednesdays and Fridays *before* your Kickboxing workouts.

ADAPTING YOUR TRAINING SCHEDULE

An important aspect of training for sports is periodization. This involves manipulating variables within a training plan in order for the athlete to achieve peak form on the day of the competition. Communicate with your

THE CHAMP'S WORKOUT (6 DAYS/WEEK FOR 6–8 WEEKS)

Shadowboxing warm-up (1 × 2-minute round)	Gradually warm up and prepare for your workout.
Shadowboxing (3 × 2-minute rounds)	Pick up the pace. Move and throw your best moves at your 'virtual opponent'. Throw your techniques with full speed and power (*see* Chapter 2).
Jump rope (continuous for 15 minutes)	Challenge yourself by adding a variety of footwork and rope moves (*see* Chapter 5).
Sparring (Monday, Wednesday and Friday: 6–10 × 2-minute rounds)	Spar between six and ten rounds to fine-tune your strategies, combinations, distancing and timing while building your endurance. Work with your sparring partner and avoid injuring each other.
Heavy bag (6–10 × 2-minute rounds)	Constantly move while throwing combinations, adding feints, slips, and weaves into the mix (*see* Chapter 3). If you've already sparred, you can perform six rounds on the heavy bag instead of ten, if preferred.
Focus pads (6 × 2-minute rounds)	Throw a wide variety of combinations, at a high level of intensity (*see* Chapter 4).
No-partner option: heavy bag ladder drill (6 minutes)	Ladder 1: throw twelve jabs, reducing down to one jab. Take a 1-minute rest. Ladder 2: throw twelve one-two punch combinations, reducing down to a single one-two punch combination.
Double-end bag (3 × 2-minute rounds)	Throw punch combination and slips (*see* Chapter 3).
Speed bag (6–8 minutes)	Strike the speed bag at a fast pace for 6–8 minutes.
Shadowboxing (3 × 2-minute rounds)	Continue working through the tiredness for another three rounds of shadowboxing to reap the benefits of improved stamina and technical awareness. Stay loose and keep moving until the end of the last round.
Stretch	Allow time to properly stretch out all the muscle groups and joint areas (*see* Chapter 8).

trainer and use discretion when following the Champ's Workout. If following the Champ's Workout and you have twelve weeks' notice before a fight, it is wise to be cautious for the first four weeks. Train well, but don't overdo it. Don't be afraid to scale back to a variation resembling the Maintenance Workout for the first four weeks. This is a great time to hone your skills and lay out your strategies, if you have access to information about your opponent. As the weeks progress, gradually increase the amount of training so you are following the Champ's Workout from eight weeks out. Continue to use discretion and alter variables according to your training performance, recovery between workouts and general well-being. It is important to get at least 7–8 hours of sleep every night. Expect to be tired often when training for a fight, but you shouldn't be sick or completely exhausted. Avoid these pitfalls through attention to detail.

There was a time when Don 'The Dragon' Wilson would fight a professional match every month or every other month. The only way to do that successfully is to be living the fighter's lifestyle '24/7'. There isn't enough time to prepare for one fight over eight weeks when following a fight schedule like this; the fighter must already be training regularly before a fight is confirmed, and can then adjust the training accordingly in preparation for the bout.

There are some adaptations you may want to make to these training plans. On your sparring days, you may want to consider reducing your heavy bag rounds in order to focus on sparring. For example, when following the Champ's Workout, there may be sparring days on which you perform just six rounds on the heavy bag in order to focus on the full ten rounds of sparring. On other sparring days, you may only do six rounds of sparring and complete ten rounds on the heavy bag instead. Mix it up, use your discretion and use these training plans as guidelines.

Taking a break

If you don't have a fight coming up and you've been training consistently week-in and week-out for a while, don't be afraid to take between four to seven days of rest from your training. This means not running in the mornings and not going to the gym to train later in the day/evening. Taking a week off training is fairly commonplace after a fight, and if you've been training consistently and are in shape, taking a week off will not negatively affect your fitness. If anything, you will be able to reap the rewards of all your training by allowing your body to *fully* recover from the work you have been putting it through on a regular basis; then you can return to training rejuvenated, invigorated and ready to continue your quest. There will be times when you're fighting regularly and you won't be able or won't want to take a week off training after a fight. Just make sure to include a few days off every twelve weeks or so. When you return to training after a full week off, ease into it for the first few days; you don't want to strain a muscle or injure something after a week of relaxing. Always perform your proper warm-ups and cool-downs, and after a few days or a week of training 'easier', slip back into your full maintenance schedule, staying ready until the next fight is scheduled.

The final bell

The life of a Professional Kickboxer is a long, tough and often lonely road. Work with a trainer and training partners whom you trust and who can assist you on your journey. Being successful with your training in the long run is dependent on your inner desire and your discipline over time. Those who aren't absolutely determined to be a champion tend to fall by the wayside fairly quickly, or they're 'on again, off again' with their training. The fighter who is determined to achieve their goals is dedicated to the sport all year round. To walk this path, you must follow at least the Maintenance Workout throughout the year until a fight is confirmed and it's time to step up your game.

TOP TEN
TOP TEN

11 DEVELOPING A WINNER'S MINDSET

Before stepping into the ring to fight, a Kickboxer must be in the correct frame of mind. In combat sports, the top athletes have supreme confidence in their abilities and are prepared to be courageous in the face of adversity. A fighter's mind cannot be clouded by self-doubt or worry about what the opponent may or may not do in the fight. The champion's mindset is founded upon confidence taken from the years of training and disciplined practice to become the best. This inner belief is unshakeable in combat.

> *The true champions are not those who never lose, but those who lose and get back up stronger than before.*
>
> *Massimo Brizi, World Champion*

No fighter is unbeatable: the greatest World Kickboxing Champions in the history of the sport have had some defeats. But these champions realized that they could be the *best* fighters if they applied themselves to the maximum in training and in competition. The champion's mindset is not to be demoralized by a defeat, but to learn from the setback and return to the ring better than ever.

OPPOSITE: Winner's mindset.

Applying the correct mindset in training, well before fighting in the ring, is what will see the aspiring Kickboxer through the numerous difficulties to be encountered on

Championship mentality.

Kickboxer's mentality versus fitness mentality

Form follows functions. If you cut corners while you are training, you will be unable to perform when it counts. Kickboxers have to push themselves to the limit when they are in training camp, so they can give maximum effort when they are fighting. Performance preparation is a day-in, day-out process in Kickboxing. A lack of preparation is the downfall of many athletes. A mentally, emotionally and physically well-prepared Kickboxer can dictate the pace of a bout, control the centre of the ring, and can also control the opponent's tactics.

the journey towards becoming a champion. Injuries, illnesses, fights cancelled, fights lost, 'life' getting in the way. These obstacles in a Kickboxer's path are normal. Those who have exceptional mental aptitude are those who overcome obstacles and succeed in their goals.

The mind controls the body.

MENTAL PREPARATION FOR COMPETITION

Before a match, a determined and motivated Kickboxer will follow extensive training regimes, both physical and mental. Many Kickboxers do this by developing routines or rituals that help them to focus their minds and block out distractions. These rituals may involve specific things such as imagery, positive thinking, and distraction- and stress-management. All of this helps to ensure that you enter a competitive situation in a positive state of mind to give your best performance. Positive imagery should be used to imagine the desired outcome of a workout, sparring session or a bout.

Attitude

> *I had a few fights where I took a pounding. It is all mental whether you slip down in your skills. Once you start to doubt yourself, you will lose. Remember that you train your ass off and your skills are honed to fight to your best. When you hit your opponent, you will hurt him, even though he might not show it. He will lose steam and confidence. Try to have fun in the ring and relax!*
>
> *Curtis Bush, World Champion*

Different fighters have different personalities: some may need to get 'psyched up' more than others. Some thrive on anger: this can sometimes work well if a fighter can channel anger effectively but can have disastrous consequences if not. Fighting 'angry' is generally not recommended; 'losing your cool' at any time during a fight will almost always cause you to make a mistake and pay a big price. Such an occurrence usually results in the 'angry' fighter either losing on points or being knocked out. Don't lose your cool.

Controlled aggression is an effective asset in the ring. You need to know when to put the pressure on, when to back off and when to breathe and reset. The ability to do this is gained through experience and time spent in the ring 'under pressure' in front of a crowd.

I relax when I fight; this makes my punches more powerful. It's all technique.... And how about the mental approach to fighting? The proper frame of mind is probably more important than most athletes would like to admit. After all, a punch is a punch, and a kick is a kick. However, if you don't have the right mentality going into a fight, forget it. You need to be positive and confident.

Don 'The Dragon' Wilson, World Champion

If you've watched Kickboxing matches live on television or via streaming services, you may have noticed that most of the top fighters stay very relaxed in the ring. Being relaxed doesn't mean to be lackadaisical or ready to fall asleep. A state of 'ready relaxation' is required in the ring: you need to instinctively make the right decisions at the right times and react to whatever the opponent may bring to the fight. Remain focused and determined, ready to fight through any level of difficulty or adversity that may come your way during the match. To do this effectively, your muscles must be relaxed, and you must maintain an inner calm; if you become flustered, you tense up, lose energy, and put yourself in a deficit. Relax and keep your psychology under control. If you tense, you inhibit your ability. If you relax, you free yourself to do your best.

Motivation and discipline

What motivates you and how strong that motivation is will ultimately determine how successful you are.... You cannot fool yourself; only you know what goes on inside that head of yours and how far you are willing to go to achieve your desires. There was never any question in my mind that I was going to be a World Champion.

'Great' Scott Ashley, World Champion

Long-term motivation is what drives success; you need a compelling reason to train and to fight as a Full Contact Kickboxer. A passion for the sport and for fighting in the ring will be instrumental in your long-term motivation. You will need a strong desire to excel and to be the best Martial Artist that you can be in order to succeed as a competitive Kickboxer.

This long-term motivation is closely related to discipline. Many people rely on short-term motivation – the 'mood of the moment' – to enable them to follow through with their plans and achieve their goals on a daily basis. However, the excitement of short-term motivation can be fleeting and unreliable. You may wake up one day and not feel like running. Is this because you're genuinely overtrained? Are you sick or injured? Be honest with yourself: if you don't want to run because you simply don't have the 'buzz' for it that day, that's not going to cut it as a good reason not to train – you have to get up and run anyway. This is what it means to be disciplined.

You may be going through a hard time in your personal life, you may have lost a fight recently and/or you may be struggling to get your next fight confirmed and arranged. Do you have the discipline to persevere and continue training to improve? Or, at the other end of the scale, your life may be going just as you'd like it to; maybe you're enjoying success, maybe you won your last fight and now your celebratory week-off from training has passed. You may not feel like training again 'just yet'. Are you going to rest on your laurels, or are you going to get back to the day-in, day-out routine of training – the same activity you approached with passion and enthusiasm

Motivation and discipline.

when you first started Kickboxing? In any of these scenarios, discipline is required to stay on course.

Discipline is a fundamental virtue of the Martial Arts and has been so throughout the decades and centuries of the development of combat skills. The discipline that becomes instilled in you through Kickboxing training will carry over into your daily life. You will be an example to others of how to be self-sufficient, of how to get things done and of how to accomplish goals, including when the 'going gets tough' or amidst the distractions of daily life. This is an example of how Martial Arts training develops exemplary members of society. The disciplined Martial Artist is a positive influence to all.

Beyond the need to be disciplined in times of distraction, difficulty or adversity, motivation should never be a problem. A Kickboxer shouldn't need much encouragement to train on a regular basis. A Kickboxer should love to train, love to fight and be highly motivated to succeed, to achieve and to accomplish lofty goals.

KICKBOXING FOR LIFE

Whether your goal is to be a champion or to improve your health and fitness through

Succeed.

Kickboxing training, all of the factors covered in this chapter will be instrumental in determining your long-term success. While Kickboxing is a fantastic and fun training approach to get you in the best shape of your life, the information pertaining to Kickboxing competitors can apply to all practitioners of the art. Just as a fighter has to run and train whether tired or not, any fitness programme can only be successful if followed consistently. You will enjoy your training for many years after you have integrated it as part of your lifestyle. Training regularly becomes more natural as time goes on, because it becomes part of your daily routine. Even when fighters retire from competition, many of them continue with their training. This is because the study of the Martial Arts is a way of life, not just fighting. The Kickboxer who applies the lessons learned through training and in competition will have the tools to lead a successful life.

Artwork by Jōnetsu.

Index